HOW TO PAY A BRIBE

Thinking Like a Criminal to Thwart Bribery Schemes

2014 Edition

ALEXANDRA WRAGE
SEVERIN WIRZ

ISBN-13: 978-1494402068
ISBN-10: 1494402068

Dedication

With my thanks to the authors who contributed their time and expertise to this book and to the world-class compliance team at TRACE: smart, committed, knowledgeable and a pleasure to have as colleagues.

Alexandra Wrage
Annapolis, Maryland

How to Pay a Bribe
Thinking Like a Criminal to Thwart Bribery Schemes

Table of Contents

About the Authors

Jeffrey D. Clark is a partner in the Litigation Department of Willkie Farr & Gallagher LLP. He represents corporations and individuals in a wide variety of criminal and civil investigations and enforcement matters, including grand jury investigations, SEC enforcement actions, and Congressional inquiries. He frequently conducts complex global internal corporate investigations and provides advice to corporate management and boards on compliance and enforcement issues. He regularly counsels companies on designing and benchmarking compliance programs and on FCPA-related matters. Mr. Clark is a former federal prosecutor with the U.S. Department of Justice and served on the Board of Directors of TRACE International and as a co-chair of the ABA Section of International Law's Anti-Corruption Committee. He is a co-author of a comprehensive treatise on the FCPA, *The Foreign Corrupt Practices Act: Compliance, Investigations, and Enforcement.*

Matteson Ellis is Special Counsel to Miller & Chevalier Chartered in Washington, DC with extensive experience in anti-corruption compliance and enforcement, including the U.S. Foreign Corrupt Practices Act. He has worked on anti-corruption matters in multiple capacities, including prevention, detection, remediation, investigation, defense, and enforcement. Mr. Ellis has performed complex, independent, and on-site internal investigations in over 20 countries throughout the Americas, Asia, Europe, and Africa considered "high corruption risk" by international monitoring organizations. He has investigated fraud and corruption and supported administrative sanctions and debarment proceedings for The World Bank and The Inter-American Development Bank. He focuses particularly on the Americas, is fluent in Spanish and Portuguese, regularly speaks on corruption matters throughout the region, and is Founder and Editor of the FCPAméricas Blog (www.fcpamericas.com).

Andrew Feinstein was elected an African National Conference (ANC) member of parliament in South Africa's first democratic elections in 1994. He resigned in 2001 in protest at the ANC government's refusal to allow an unfettered investigation into an arms deal that was tainted by allegations of high-level corruption. His political memoir, *After the Party: A personal and political journey inside the ANC,* was published in 2007. His second, critically acclaimed book *The Shadow World: Inside the Global Arms Trade,* was first published by Penguin and Farrar, Straus & Giroux in late 2011. He appears regularly in a range of print and broadcast media.

Kathleen Hamann is a partner in the white collar practice at White & Case LLP, specializing in anticorruption matters and transnational and extraterritorial criminal law. She previously was the longest-tenured prosecutor in the FCPA Unit of the Department of Justice, where she was a trial attorney and Anticorruption Policy Counsel. She oversaw the industry-wide investigation into transnational bribery in the medical device and pharmaceutical industries. Before her time at the Department of Justice, Ms. Hamann was a Foreign Service Officer at the Department of State for more than ten years, focusing on anticorruption and transnational law enforcement cooperation.

Paul Holden is a South African-born and London-based historian, researcher, writer and activist. He has published four books to date on issues related to corruption, governance and democratic practice in South Africa. Two of his books – *The Arms Deal in Your Pocket* (2008) and *Who Rules South Africa* (2012) – were major national best-sellers. His major investigative work to date was the book *The Devil in the Detail: How the Arms Deal Changed Everything* (2011), which collated the result of years of detailed investigation into South Africa's biggest post-apartheid scandal. He has appeared regularly on South African and international news platforms discussing issues related to corruption and its impact on development and democratisation in developing countries.

Musikilu Mojeed is Managing Editor at Nigeria's multimedia newspaper, *Premium Times*. Until 2011, he was Investigative Editor at Nigeria's *NEXT* newspaper where he directed the groundbreaking investigative work of that newspaper and coordinated the paper's WikiLeaks coverage. Mr. Mojeed is also a recent J.S. Knight Journalism Fellow at Stanford University. Before then, he was a Ford Foundation International Fellow at The City University of New York. He has reported extensively on corruption, human rights and human trafficking in Africa.

Barnaby Pace is a writer and investigator on corruption and conflict issues. He was the primary researcher for *Shadow World: Inside the Global Arms Trade*, co-author of "Sins of Commission," the lead chapter for the *SIPRI Yearbook 2011*, and has worked for a range of NGOs and media outlets. He is a member of the steering committees of the UK based Campaign Against Arms Trade and Forceswatch. He has appeared as a commentator on Sky News, BBC, Al Jazeera and Russia Today. He also tweets @pace_nik and blogs at armouersfaith.wordpress.com.

Ken Silverstein is a Washington-based investigative reporter. He was the Washington editor for *Harper's Magazine* from 2006 to 2010. Between 2002 and 2006, Mr. Silverstein worked on the investigative unit of *The Los Angeles Times'* Washington bureau. He has written for *Foreign Policy, Slate, Salon, Mother Jones, The Nation, Wallpaper, London Review of Books, Book Forum* and many other publications.

Daniel Jordan Smith joined the Department of Anthropology at Brown University in July 2001. He received an AB in Sociology from Harvard University in 1983, an MPH from Johns Hopkins University in 1989, and a PhD in Anthropology from Emory University in 1999. Smith conducts research in Nigeria focusing on a range of issues, including social change, political culture, kinship, and health. He won the 2008 Margaret Mead Award for his book, *A Culture of Corruption: Everyday Deception and Popular Discontent in Nigeria* (Princeton University Press, 2007). His newest book, *AIDS Doesn't Show Its Face: Inequality, Morality, and Social Change in Nigeria* (University of Chicago Press, 2014) examines the social effects of Nigeria's HIV epidemic.

Amy L. Sommers is a partner with the law firm K&L Gates in Shanghai. Her fluency in both Mandarin and English, and her understanding of the economic system and culture of China and its Western trading partners enhance the value of Ms. Sommer's advice to her clients. Her areas of expertise include a variety of strategic business and commercial transactions such as real estate, mergers and acquisitions, commercial financing and investment in China's highly regulated economy. A significant portion of her practice involves advising on US Foreign Corrupt Practices Act and PRC antibribery compliance. Her published works include "China Adopts Amendments to the Criminal Law to Outlaw Bribery of Foreign Officials" in the *National Law Review*, "The Amended Law to the Company Law of the People's Republic of China (PRC): Encouraging Foreign Investment, Strengthening Shareholder Protections," in the *Bloomberg Corporate Law Journal* (co-author), and "A Lawyer's Survival Guide to Shanghai," published in *International Law News*. In 2007, Ms. Sommers won the Business Woman of the Year award of the Expatriate Professional Women's Society in Shanghai. Ms. Sommers is honored to serve as a member of the board of directors of TRACE International, Inc.

Alexandra Wrage is the president of TRACE International. She has written three compliance guidebooks and is the author of *Bribery and Extortion: Undermining Business, Governments and Security*, and the host of the training DVD *Toxic Transactions: Bribery, Extortion and the High Price of Bad Business* produced by NBC. Ms. Wrage has previously served on the Independent Governance Committee (IGC) of the Fédération Internationale de Football Association (FIFA), and as Chair of the Anti-Corruption Committee of the ABA's International Section, and Chair of the International Legal Affairs Committee of the Association of Corporate Counsel. She has also participated in anti-bribery working groups with the OECD and the UN Global Compact. Ms. Wrage was named one of the "Canadians Changing the World" by the *Toronto Globe and Mail* in 2011, and one of Maryland's Top 100 Women for 2012.

Preface to the 2014 Edition

Severin Wirz

This book arises from one simple premise — that the key to identifying and finding corruption is knowing what it looks like. But truly understanding corruption at more than just a surface level is no easy task. Those who perpetuate bribery schemes are masters of subterfuge, and often go to great lengths to keep their machinations hidden from public view. They delete emails, forge records, set up fake bank accounts and use code words in their communications with one another. Everything they do is designed to make that which is illicit look completely normal: nothing to see here, just move on.

Even when a bribery scheme is discovered, the ensuing government investigation often reveals only the most cursory of details. Basic human interactions are muddled in legal jargon. Instead of learning the inner goings-on of a criminal rendezvous, we get "Consultant A promised to make payment to Government Official B in order to obtain or retain business for Company C." Certainly not good beach reading.

Given that so few foreign bribery cases actually make it to trial, where the facts might come to light, how are we to lay bare the ways in which corruption actually functions in the real world? In this second edition of *How to Pay a Bribe: Thinking Like a Criminal to Thwart Bribery Schemes*, we've recruited the help of those who come closest to understanding these bribery schemes without actually being involved in them. These are the authors, researchers and investigative journalists whose stories are able to breathe life into the corruption literature. They are also the practicing lawyers and former prosecutors who have investigated these bribery schemes first hand.

We have made an effort to reflect a diversity of geographic views, with experts who specialize in Latin America, Europe, Africa and Asia. What unites each story is their wonderful attention to detail, revealing the human side behind so many of these schemes. Behind every case is a story involving the decisions that real people make. We hope that as you read these stories, you find them not only educational as cautionary tales, but engaging too, and that they provide better clarity as to how to recognize corruption in your own organization.

Introduction

Alexandra Wrage

A great deal has been written about the cost of corruption and the pace of anti-bribery enforcement. The cost is now recognized to be far greater than was originally feared, impacting the poorest most dramatically. Corruption is theft by those in a position of power. It may be the power of a petty tyrant whose domain is a tiny customs office at a remote port or of a grasping bureaucrat who wields the official stamp for a license of little significance. Alternatively, it may be the power of a kleptocrat sitting atop the corrupt regime of an oil-rich nation with one hand in the country's till and the other in the pockets of foreign multinationals trying to operate there. In either case, the local citizens suffer because their official representatives, elected or otherwise, serve their own interests rather than the interests of the larger community.

In response to this global scourge, the pace of enforcement has picked up steeply in the last few years. Although the United States still holds all of the records for number of enforcement actions, size of financial penalties and length of prison terms, other jurisdictions are very much in the fray. But how the bribes are actually paid has received too little attention. Those seeking to deter and detect bribes need to understand how value is generated, disguised and transferred. In order to train effectively, anti-bribery lawyers should work with plausible scenarios that resonate with the audience.

This book has been written for in-house counsel and others keen to train their colleagues to avoid bribery, in the best case, and to uncover bribery schemes when others are determined to use bribes as a part of their business strategy. In-house counsel and compliance officers and other anti-bribery practitioners can learn from one another. The imagination of even very creative criminals is finite. To continue the conversation, we encourage you to share your own stories with us by writing to HowtoPayaBribe@TRACEinternational.org. We hope to incorporate many of these in future editions.

Chapter One

"Hard to Draw a Line" — Glencore, Commodity Trading and Corruption

Ken Silverstein

Bribery can be a way of doing business for some companies. When that becomes the culture of a company, it can be very difficult to change. In the case described below, we see how for one such company, Glencore, the high-risk market of commodity trading has lent itself to a lax attitude allowing for obtuse and potentially improper business transactions.

When Glencore, the world's biggest commodities brokerage firm, went public in May 2011, the company was initially valued at nearly $60 billion — more than Boeing or Ford Motor Co. At the time, the company controlled over half the international tradable market in zinc and copper and about a third of the world's seaborne coal; it was one of the world's largest grain exporters, with about 9 percent of the global market; and it handled 3 percent of daily global oil consumption for customers ranging from state-owned energy companies in Brazil and India to American multinationals like ExxonMobil and Chevron. The firm posted revenues of $186 billion in 2011, employed some 55,000 people in at least 40 countries, and generated a 38 percent return on equity.

Since its Initial Public Offering (IPO), the company has only gotten more immense in scale by making a series of acquisitions, including a takeover of mining giant Xstrata. GlencoreXstrada, as the company is now known, trades, manufactures, refines, ships, or stores at least 90 commodities in dozens of countries. "Wherever you turn in the world of commodities, you bump into Glencore," says Nicholas Shaxson, author of *Treasure Islands*, a book about tax havens, and an associate fellow at the British think tank Chatham House. "It is twice as big as Koch industries and it has an unhealthy grip on some of the world's most important commodity markets, with influence that stretches from Texas to Tehran to Taipei."

The massive new wealth generated by Glencore's IPO turned nearly 500 employees into overnight multimillionaires and made billionaires of at least five senior executives, including CEO Ivan Glasenberg. "We are not going to change the way we operate," he vowed. "Being public will have absolutely no effect on the business."

From a business stand point that declaration makes sense, given Glencore's historic success and profitability. From the standpoint of best business practices and transparency, though, Glasenberg's vow was cause for concern.

Ever since being founded in 1974, Glencore has operated in markets that scare off more risk-averse companies that fear running afoul of extraterritorial corporate governance laws in the United States and the European Union. In fact, those markets are precisely what Deutsche Bank, in a pre-IPO assessment, identified as Glencore's "key drivers" of profitability: copper in the Democratic Republic of the Congo, coal in Colombia, oil and natural gas in Equatorial Guinea, and gold in Kazakhstan.

All those countries mix extraordinary natural wealth and various degrees of political instability, violence, and strongman leaders. Glencore's experience and adeptness operating in these "frontier regions" and "challenging political jurisdictions" — Deutsche Bank's delicate euphemisms for countries known for corruption, autocracy, and human rights abuses — is central, the investment firm wrote, to Glencore's "significant growth potential."

But the real secret to Glencore's historic success has been working with shady intermediaries who help the company gain access to resources and curry favor with the corrupt, resource-rich regimes that have made Glencore so fabulously wealthy. Given the nature of its business, that may be the only way for a company like Glencore to thrive. "Unlike the case with many industries, minerals and energy are often owned by the state in Third World countries," says Michael Ross, author of *The Oil Curse* and a professor at the University of California, Los Angeles. "And in a number of countries where Glencore operates, doing business means putting money into the pockets of repressive governments and corrupt rulers. In some of those places…it's hard to draw a line between what's legally corrupt and what's not."

Switzerland: Where the rules do not apply

Commodity brokers and oil traders have flocked to Switzerland ever since the industry boomed in the mid-1970s, following the first Arab oil boycott of Israel. The reasons for that choice are numerous, among them the country's long record as a financial and tax haven that offers strict rules on bank and corporate secrecy, and its weak business regulation. For years, Swiss authorities did not prosecute bribery, and banks were not subject to money-laundering laws. Some rules have been tightened but commodity traders and financial intermediaries are still largely unregulated. "It's a light touch here," one Swiss trader told me during a reporting trip to the country. "There are rules but they are not always applied."[1]

Among the hundred of companies who are based or have major operations in Geneva, are American corporate behemoths like Cargill, state energy firms from Ukraine and Azerbaijan, and the trading houses of multinationals like Total of France. Independent traders represented in Switzerland include Vitol, one of Glencore's biggest rivals, which pled guilty for paying illegal commissions to Saddam Hussein's government under the United Nations Oil-for-Food program and Trafigura, which gained notoriety in 2006 when it illegally dumped 400 tons of toxic waste in the Ivory Coast. Trafigura subsequently paid a $200 million fine to settle charges stemming from the case, which resulted in ten deaths and tens of thousands of illnesses.

Uniquely among the giant trading firms, Glencore is located in Zug, a charming canton a few hours from Geneva and just north of the Alps. Zug's population of residents and registered companies both hover around 27,000, and the corporate tax rate averages around 15 percent, low even by Swiss standards.

---

[1] Like other traders I met, he would talk only on the condition that I not reveal his name.

The conventional view of oil traders is that they make money by leveraging information to buy cheap and sell high. They are, Daniel Yergin writes in his book *The Quest*, "nimble players who... with hair-trigger timing, dart in and out to take advantage of the smallest anomalies and mispricings."

Yet all of the traders I talked to acknowledged that political connections were even more vital than technical expertise. "You can be the smartest trader in the world and you still can't make money without access to oil," one told me. "Fortunately, there is always access if you are willing to pay enough cash."

Another trader, who worked for Glencore in Africa, said that payoffs to government officials used to be pretty straightforward, but had become more sophisticated over the years. "Ten years ago, I'd get on a plane with money straight from the bank to spread around," he told me forthrightly. "Now you sign a contract with an offshore company that's owned by the relative of some government official you need. The company may not be strictly legitimate or conduct any real business for you, but everybody's happy."

Business Model: "Systemic bribes and kickbacks"

Leveraging ties to dictators and spreading profits around were at the heart of Glencore's business model after Marc Rich, a Belgian-born U.S. citizen, founded its predecessor company in 1974. Rich started in 1954 as a mail clerk at Philipp Brothers, then the world's dominant commodities firm, and within two years had worked his way into the position of junior trader. He left Philipp Brothers in 1974 and established Marc Rich & Co. in the canton of Zug. From early on, Rich cultivated ties to monarchs and presidents, diplomats and intelligence agencies, especially Iran's SAVAK under the Shah. He also worked closely with Israel's Mossad and brokered a deal by which Iran secretly supplied oil to the Jewish state.

Rich, who died in 2013, used offshore front companies and corporate cutouts to try to stay below the radar. He also pioneered the practice of commodity swaps, like the uranium-for-oil deals he brokered in the 1980s between apartheid South Africa and Islamic Iran and Soviet Russia. Such deals frequently caused him trouble with U.S. authorities, and in 1983 Rich fled his home in New York to Switzerland just before the Justice Department issued an indictment against him on charges of racketeering, illegal trading with Iran, and tax evasion. The House Committee on Government Reform later described his business as "based largely on systematic bribes and kickbacks to corrupt local officials."

Still, Rich continued to thrive until he unsuccessfully tried to corner the global zinc market in 1992 and nearly bankrupted the firm with $172 million in losses, at which point he was forced out in a management buyout. The new directors renamed the company Glencore, short for Global Energy Commodities and Resources.[2]

Rich retired to a lavish estate on the shores of Lake Lucerne, but the new Glencore, like the old one, relied on a network of fixers, middlemen, and business partners who gain special access to key decision-makers in the countries where it operates. In one post-Rich example, the company profited handsomely by dealing with Saddam Hussein under the 1996-2003 U.N. Oil-for-Food Program, which allowed the Iraqi dictator to trade limited quantities of oil in exchange for humanitarian supplies.

The U.N.'s Independent Inquiry Committee reported in 2005 that Hussein had awarded special "allocations" to companies and individuals who were friendly to the regime. A Glencore agent, Pakistani businessman Murtaza Lakhani, was a conspicuous regime sycophant who hosted a peace concert at his local villa just weeks before the 2003 U.S. invasion. The U.N. committee raised questions about lavish commissions Glencore paid Lakhani.

The Iraq Survey Group, the U.S.-led fact-finding mission sent after the invasion, concluded that Glencore was "one of the most active purchasers" of oil under the Oil-for-Food Program and had paid $3,222,780 in "illegal surcharges." Yet Glencore was not charged in the scandal after claiming it was unaware surcharges were being paid and that Lakhani's high fees reflected the extra risk of doing business with Iraq, not slush money for bribes.

Rich admitted that the old Glencore paid bribes. The new Glencore, however, denies doing so: "We will not be complicit in any third party's violation of the law in any country, nor the payment nor receipt of bribes, nor participate in any other criminal, fraudulent or corrupt practice," reads the company's corporate practice statement.

---

[2] On Bill Clinton's last day in office, the president granted Rich a controversial pardon stemming from the 18-year-old indictment; critics argued that the pardon was connected to the generous contributions that Rich's ex-wife, Denise, made to a variety of Democratic causes.

Nonetheless, investigations over the past decade have alleged that Glencore's agents and employees made illegal payments to secure market access in a number of countries. In 2009, U.S. and Bahraini prosecutors investigated allegations that Glencore's employees had made $4.6 million in improper payments to executives at Aluminium Bahrain, a state-owned smelter, to secure below-market prices on aluminum products. Glencore denied the allegations; in 2009 it paid Aluminium Bahrain an out-of-court settlement of $20 million.

In 2012, a court in Belgium found that a Glencore employee paid a European Union official for inside information that allowed it to win millions of dollars in cereal contracts. Glencore reportedly provided the official with a vacation worth more than $600,000 on the French Riviera. It also bought him a cell phone and picked up $4,000 worth of calls he made to the company, some placed just minutes before bid deadlines.

Operating in the Frontier: Middlemen Needed

In the "frontier" areas where Glencore thrives, doing business is all but impossible without a well-connected political patron who has intimate connections to senior-level decision-makers. "We conduct whatever due diligence is appropriate in each situation to ensure we operate in line with Glencore Corporate Practice," the company's then-spokesman, Simon Buerk, told me in 2012 when I asked how the firm vetted its business partners and local representatives.

However, Glencore's patrons along the frontier have often been hugely controversial and questions have frequently been raised about how they became so close to government officials. A case in point is its partner in the Democratic Republic of the Congo (DRC), Dan Gertler, an Israeli businessman known for his intimate ties to President Joseph Kabila. The DRC is the poster child of the resource-cursed failed state but it has irresistible appeal to companies like Glencore due to its vast mineral deposits.

The grandson of the founder of the Israel Diamond Exchange, Gertler turned up in the Congo in 1997 at age 23, as the country was descending into a hellish war that left at least 4 million dead. Gertler had few contacts when he arrived in the Congo, and a confidential report by the international investigative firm Kroll described him as having a "poor record in fulfilling promised investments." But he did have something that a government at war desperately needed: cash. Three years after he arrived in the Congo, the government — then headed by Laurent Kabila, Joseph's father, who was assassinated in 2001 — sold Gertler a monopoly on diamond sales for $20 million, though it was reportedly worth hundreds of millions of dollars.

In the Congo, Gertler's diamond monopoly became politically controversial and was cancelled months after Joseph Kabila came to power. Still, he continued to land profitable deals afterward. Public records and documents released in late-2011 by a British parliamentarian show that the Congolese government secretly sold vast mining assets on the cheap to various British Virgin Islands-registered shell companies, several of which are linked to Gertler.

Shimon Cohen, Gertler's London-based public relations advisor, told me that Gertler's family trusts had invested or brought over $2 billion of investment into the mining sector in the Congo over the past 15 years. He said Gertler took risks operating in the Congo and that the deals were straightforward business transactions. Gertler, he acknowledged, enjoyed "a close friendship with the president." Indeed, he was one of the few Westerners invited to Joseph Kabila's 2006 wedding, and in June 2011 he joined the president on the VIP tribune during Independence Day celebrations.

For his part, Gertler has called Kabila "the most promising new president in the world — a new Mandela." That's not a view shared by most observers. The U.S. State Department's 2012 human rights report reports a long list of problems in Kabila's Congo, among them "impunity throughout the country for many serious abuses, including unlawful killings, disappearances, torture, rape, and arbitrary arrests and detention," and "widespread official corruption."

With help from Gertler, Glencore won a $4.5 billion stake in the Congo with multiple holdings. One former Glencore employee described the company and Gertler as "totally enmeshed" in the Congo. Gertler, this person told me, "managed the entire relationship between Glencore and Kabila and the Congolese government," with Glasenberg, the CEO, flying into Kinshasa or Lubumbashi on a private jet to meet with him.

For understandable reasons, Glencore was never keen to advertise its relationship with Gertler. It did, however, offer him a series of discreet, complex, and remarkably profitable deals. In one case, Glencore sold stock in a Congolese mining company it owned at roughly 60 percent of its market value to Ellesmere Global Limited, a British Virgin Islands firm whose ultimate owner was a Gertler-family trust. Ellesmere quickly sold it back to Glencore at close to full market price, netting a profit of about $26 million.

However much Gertler made through his firms' deals with Glencore, Glencore has clearly profited too, given the huge portfolio it accumulated in Congo. "Glencore has a Gertler everywhere," a former Glencore employee told me. "That's standard."

In Russia, Glencore's chief sponsor has been oilman Mikhail Gutseriev, who in 1995 was elected to the Duma as a member of right-wing nationalist Vladimir Zhirinovsky's party. Gutseriev also owned a bank and casino, and he was running a newly created tax-free business zone in Ingushetia, a small, violence-ridden republic bordering soon-to-be-war-torn Chechnya. In her book *Sale of the Century*, Chrystia Freeland described his Moscow offices as decorated in gold, crystal, and floral designs that "an eight-year-old girl with a princess fantasy and a gold credit card might concoct."

In the mid-2000s, Gutseriev patched together a number of small energy companies into RussNeft, which later became one of Russia's biggest oil companies. He was understatedly described in a U.S. diplomatic cable released by WikiLeaks as "not known for his transparent corporate governance," though he certainly did well for himself. Gutseriev has regularly appeared on Forbes's list of the richest Russians, with a fortune estimated in 2012 at around $6.7 billion.

But Gutseriev's meteoric rise to full-fledged oligarch status was only possible due to massive assistance from Glencore's hidden hand. Business contracts I obtained show the company financed RussNeft's "spectacular growth" and "aggressive acquisition strategy" — as one confidential 2005 Glencore document put it — at every step. Glencore, the document said, "appreciates his acquisitive nature and ability to identify good assets in a short space of time."

In return for its funding, Glencore got an exclusive deal to market RussNeft's oil, won the right to appoint senior personnel, and ended up with about half the equity in four oil production subsidiaries. "Glencore associated with him because he could buy physical assets in Russia and it couldn't," one well-placed source told me.

Glencore has also done well in Kazakhstan, another country that can be treacherous terrain for foreign investors. A U.S. Commerce Department report warns of "burdensome regulations that often reflect a way of doing business that is reminiscent of the Soviet Union." Glencore's local sponsor there is oligarch Bulat Utemuratov, who has partnered in mineral deals with Glencore through his firm Verny Capital.

A former head of Kazakhstan's powerful National Security Committee who once held a top position in the ruling party and served as chief of staff to dictator Nursultan Nazarbayev between 2006 and 2008, Utemuratov is known among insiders as the president's "consigliere," a Western expert on Kazakhstan told me. "You can't do any large-scale business in Kazakhstan without the president's approval, and you can't get that without direct access to the president, which Utemuratov gets for you," the person said.

So will going public alter Glencore's business model over the long term? The company's culture goes totally against it, the former Glencore trader I interviewed told me. "That's just not the way traders work," especially, he added, Glencore.

Ken Silverstein is a Washington-based investigative reporter. He was the Washington editor for *Harper's Magazine* from 2006 to 2010. Between 2002 and 2006, Mr. Silverstein worked on the investigative unit of The *Los Angeles Times'* Washington bureau. He has written for *Foreign Policy, Slate, Salon, Mother Jones, The Nation, Wallpaper, London Review of Books, Book Forum* and many other publications.

Chapter Two

Balancing Business and Compliance

Jeffrey D. Clark

In this fictionalized account, a rising star at a struggling company feels pressure to finalize a key international deal in a new emerging market. Feeling the squeeze from all angles, he pushes ahead on the contract even in the face of obvious compliance red flags. This story closely mirrors real life scenarios in which we see how inadequate "tone from top" can truly spread like a cancer to various levels of a company – ruining not only the company's business opportunities, but also endangering the well-being of its employees.

United Insurance International ("UII") was a sprawling international insurance and financial services company. Having struggled in recent years to find significant growth opportunities in the mature markets in the United States and Western Europe, UII identified the emerging markets, and particularly those in the Asia-Pacific region, as a key area for strategic growth. That made UII's Emerging Markets Division ("EMD"), and particularly its AsiaPac region, the focus of senior management attention. As a demonstration of its commitment to the region, UII senior management appointed Asef Choudhry to lead EMD's efforts in AsiaPac. Choudhry was recognized within the company as a rising star. In communicating the appointment to Choudhry, the Senior Vice President for the Eastern Hemisphere made it clear that this was a big opportunity; if Choudhry could produce bottom line results by the end of the next fiscal year, this position would be a stepping stone to a major promotion and a fast track to UII's executive ranks. The senior manager let Choudhry know that he understood that doing business in this part of the world was difficult, but he was confident that Choudhry would overcome any obstacles he might encounter.

One of the biggest opportunities in the AsiaPac region was in the Philippines, where the Ministry of Finance had announced its intention to assemble a panel of insurance companies that would serve as the primary insurers for all state run commercial enterprises. Choudhry saw this as a key deal – UII had no presence in the Philippines and had never been able to get a foothold in the market. He put his most aggressive business development manager, Raul Cruz, on it.

Cruz attacked the project with great enthusiasm. Within weeks he was able to get a meeting with the Minister of Finance. Choudhry and Cruz gave a presentation explaining UII's expertise, stability, financial strength, and long record of success in other parts of the world. Both thought the presentation went well; they had given it their best shot. But weeks, then several months, went by and they heard nothing. Cruz's calls to the ministry went unanswered. They knew from public announcements and industry rumor that the insurance tender was proceeding as scheduled. Finally Cruz got a call from someone on the Minister's staff. The staffer told Cruz that the Minister had appreciated the presentation and that UII's expertise and financial strength were beyond question, but the Minister was not convinced that UII had a true commitment to doing business in the Philippines. Despite Cruz's attempts to provide assurances, the staffer was unimpressed. He told Cruz that the other international insurance companies competing to get on the panel had overcome this kind of perception problem by partnering with local companies. He mentioned that there were several such companies that would make suitable partners, but that Omicron Advisors stood out as one of the best. Omicron, he said, had the connections and credibility to shore up UII's bid.

Cruz made some discreet inquiries about Omicron and discovered that the company was run by a childhood friend of the Minister. The company had contracts across a wide range of industries, from oil and gas to telecommunications to shipping. It was known for its access to the upper-most reaches of government and for its ability to deliver results. To Cruz, Omicron sounded perfect. But time was running short. The tender deadline was only weeks away. Cruz contacted Choudhry, who had been riding him hard to show results in the Philippines. He described to Choudhry his conversation with the ministry staffer and the word on the street about Omicron. He told Choudhry that Omicron was UII's last chance for success in the Philippines tender. Choudhry gave his approval to proceed and told Cruz that he would put a call into AsiaPac compliance to let them know that EMD would be submitting a consultant for expedited approval. Mindful of UII's somewhat cumbersome and notorious slow due diligence process, Choudhry directed Cruz to take charge of the process by issuing a standard due diligence questionnaire to Omicron and commissioning a business intelligence report. Simultaneously, Cruz was to begin to negotiate with Omicron the terms of their commercial arrangement.

Cruz and Choudhry leapt into action. Cruz spearheaded the due diligence. After several exchanges with Omicron, he was able to get them to answer most of the questions, but there were a few sticking points. Omicron was a British Virgin Islands company and insisted that by law it was not required to disclose its owners. It would provide only the name and address of the BVI law firm that served as the company's registered agent. The business intelligence report also presented some potential issues. The public records information, though minimal, was fine. But the human source intelligence was more ambiguous. Omicron was not known to have any experience in the insurance industry. It was rumored to be owned by the Minister of Finance but the business intelligence firm noted that some of the sources may have had a political axe to grind and that such rumors of corrupt activities were common in the Philippines.

For his part, Choudhry called the AsiaPac compliance lead, Tian Xu, to alert him to the time-sensitive request. Choudhry stressed the critical nature of the opportunity and that senior management was watching the deal very closely and wanted to see it get done. In light of this, and in view of the time constraints, he told Xu that he had authorized Cruz to take the lead in gathering due diligence information and instructed Cruz to provide compliance with a summary of the pertinent information. He forewarned that EMD would need compliance to turn the file around with an approval in no more than two days. Xu, who had been in his position for only two months, was slightly uncomfortable with this arrangement, so he checked in with his boss, the Vice President for AsiaPac. She told him that she was aware of the business priority of the Philippines opportunity and that compliance, and Xu in particular, was there to support the business, so he should show some flexibility in the process.

Meanwhile, Cruz's efforts to settle the commercial terms were proving difficult. UII preferred to pay consultants on a fixed-fee basis. In the relatively rare occasion in which the company agreed to pay a consultant on a commission basis, it usually paid commissions of between 5 and 8 percent of its revenue on the transaction. Omicron was insisting on a commission of 35% and would not budge from that number. This bothered Cruz and Choudhry, since a commission of that size would eat into the margins on the deal. Choudhry directed Cruz to explore other options for a local consultant, but Cruz reported back that all of the international companies competing for the panel had engaged local consultants. Omicron was thought to have the inside track and, in any event, all of the other realistic options had already aligned with other international companies. There was no one left who could deliver results. Reluctantly, Choudhry told Cruz to agree to the 35% commission.

To streamline the contracting process, Choudhry authorized Cruz to enter into a binding letter of intent, with a formal contract to be put in place after the tender award. Cruz reported back that Omicron rejected this approach, saying that the signed contract had to be submitted with the bid. This was nowhere in the bid documents, but Omicron insisted that it was local practice and would be the only way for UII to get "credit" for its local partnership. With only a week to go until the bid deadline, there was no way to get the Omicron contract, particularly with its unusual terms, through UII's full contracting process. Out of options and having come this far, Choudhry agreed to sign the contract. "When we win the bid," he thought, "this will just be an administrative detail. And besides, sometimes it is better to ask for forgiveness than permission."

The last hurdle remaining was regional compliance. Choudhry was not about to let this young compliance officer stand in his way. He had Cruz summarize the due diligence performed, but made sure that the sticking points were carefully worded. The summary stated that Omicron's ownership was a BVI company with no red flags and that further inquiries were prohibited by local law. With regard to the business intelligence report, the summary indicated that Omicron was a known local entity in good standing and that only a few vague negative comments came to light, primarily from those whose credibility was suspect. The summary did not note the specific commission agreed to but stated only that the commercial terms were "in accord with local market conditions." The summary also did not note that the contract had already been signed, but Choudhry called Xu before Cruz submitted the summary. He told Xu that under local practice, nothing short of a signed contract would demonstrate sufficiently UII's commitment to a long-term presence in the Philippines. Choudhry also told Xu that he was authorized by senior management to enter the agreement and that the compliance sign-off was just a "pro forma" exercise to complete the file. With that, Xu responded to Cruz's email summary of the due diligence within minutes with a simple, "OK."

Three days after UII's bid was submitted along with the signed contract with Omicron, Cruz was arrested by Philippines authorities as he re-entered the country after a trip to Singapore regional headquarters. The tender process had been declared null and void and the Minister of Finance had been accused publicly of corruption. Two days later, following an article in the Wall Street Journal describing the scandal and the arrest of a UII employee by local authorities, UII was contacted by the DOJ and SEC.

Compliance Lessons

There is plenty that went wrong in this story. To begin with, it seems that the compliance tone at UII is lacking at all levels. The senior vice president put pressure on Choudhry to produce results and seemed to condition a future promotion on those results. Although he gave lip service to the challenges of doing business in the AsiaPac region, he made it clear that Choudhry should "overcome" any obstacles to achieve success. All businesses can and should expect results from their managers, but this kind of "succeed at all costs" message in a difficult environment sets a dangerous tone, making ethical and compliance concerns an after-thought. This tone from senior management permitted, if not encouraged, Choudhry to act improperly.

A company's tone is set not just at the top but, equally important, in "the middle." Perhaps following the cues from his superior, Choudhry adopted a succeed-at-all-costs mentality. He proceeded to use Omicron as an agent in the face of patent red flags: the company was recommended by the Ministry of Finance; it was rumored to be owned by a childhood friend of the Minister (or perhaps by the Minister himself); it refused to disclose its owners, hiding behind the fact that it was registered in the BVI; the proposed commission was more than three times UII's usual commission rate; and Omicron insisted that its contract with UII be submitted with the bid as proof of UII's "commitment" to the Philippines. Choudhry and Cruz together withheld key information from the compliance manager, Xu, and lied outright by saying that he had already been authorized by senior management to enter into the agreement with Omicron.

The compliance function at UII also failed to fulfill its role. Compliance should have been involved early on in the process of vetting the potential consultant in the Philippines and had an active role in the process. Instead, Xu let Choudhry and Cruz dictate and control the process and accepted Cruz's (inaccurate) summary of information gathered in the due diligence process. Xu should have insisted on seeing for himself the questionnaire provided by Omicron, the business intelligence report, and any other due diligence information UII had gathered. He accepted without question that Omicron did not have to disclose its ownership because it was a BVI company. Whether Omicron is required under BVI law to publicly disclose its shareholders is an entirely different question than whether it will choose to disclose its ownership to a commercial counter-party. Xu also failed to understand the commercial terms of the relationship, accepting the ambiguous statement that the terms were "in accord with local market conditions." Often key information necessary to assess compliance risks in a proposed third party relationship exists within the company itself. It is the obligation of compliance to find and conduct an objective review of that information. Finally, the relatively inexperienced Xu let himself be intimidated and bullied by Choudhry. In the end, after receiving insufficient, summary information, he issued a weak "OK" only minutes after receiving the information.

Xu's unwillingness to challenge the business on the Omicron relationship was compounded by the fact that his immediate supervisor, a regional business manager rather than an independent compliance professional, gave him no support. When Xu expressed his discomfort with the Omicron arrangement, his supervisor did not support a further inquiry but, rather, reinforced that the deal was important, that his job was to support the business, and he should be "flexible." Although Xu could have raised his concerns elsewhere within the organization, it is not surprising that he did not, given the structure of the reporting relationships and the attitude of the business personnel. He had little reason to expect support in pressing his compliance concerns.

Beyond the failings of compliance, it appears that UII may have other internal controls deficiencies. For example, Choudhry was able to obtain and enter a contract without the involvement of the law department. Even where compliance is a separate function, the law department has a vital control function to play. In this case, employees should not be able to draft and enter into sensitive, high-risk contracts without the counsel and approval of the law department. The involvement of a lawyer could have provided much needed support for Xu and provided a second set of eyes — independent of the business team — on the terms of the deal.

Business organizations are not in business to be compliant, they are in business to make money. But a business that pursues short-sighted efforts to succeed at all costs without regard to compliance will fail in the long run. Business managers must recognize and communicate to employees throughout their organization that compliance officers are not obstacles to be overcome but partners to ensure that the business's success is sustainable in the long term. UII learned that lesson the hard way.

Jeffrey D. Clark is a partner in the Litigation Department of Willkie Farr & Gallagher LLP. He represents corporations and individuals in a wide variety of criminal and civil investigations and enforcement matters, including grand jury investigations, SEC enforcement actions, and Congressional inquiries. He regularly counsels companies on designing and benchmarking compliance programs and on FCPA-related matters. Mr. Clark is a former federal prosecutor with the U.S. Department of Justice and served on the Board of Directors of TRACE International and as a co-chair of the ABA Section of International Law's Anti-Corruption Committee. He is a co-author of a comprehensive treatise on the FCPA, *The Foreign Corrupt Practices Act: Compliance, Investigations, and Enforcement.*

Chapter Three

Not Such Lone Sharks: Bribery and Corruption in the Russia-Angola Debt Deal

Andrew Feinstein and Paul Holden

This article is based on a report published by Corruption Watch UK (of which the authors are directors) in 2013 entitled 'The Corrupt Angola-Russia Debt Deal.' A full referenced version of the report, along with the underlying documents on which it was based, can be downloaded from www.cw-uk.org.

Two countries with a long history of grand corruption, politicians and officials already worth millions if not billions, two controversial arms dealers, a Swiss bank and a clandestine debt transaction: An opportunity for bribery? Surely not!

The Russian-Angola Debt Deal is replete not only with rarefied jargon, a plethora of institutional acronyms and arcane financial calculations, but also with intrigue and drama in spades. And like all good international intrigue, there were pots of cash exchanged: over $386 million alone to Angolan politicians and middlemen.

Struck in 1996 between the governments of Angola and Russia to settle historical debts between the two countries incurred during the Cold War and after, the Deal is the archetype of a transaction structured, from its conception, to enrich a handful of shady characters and the political elite of at least one of the negotiating countries. Swaddled in the snug embrace of legal documents, the crime was hidden in plain sight, codified into the agreements that underpinned it. Taking place in multiple jurisdictions (a large percentage of which were tax havens), the Deal required the assistance of numerous banking institutions and intermediaries, all of whom aided and abetted the crimes, either through negligence or active complicity. Perpetrated by larger-than-life characters with fingers in numerous questionable pies, it attracted the attention of both the media and international law enforcement. Despite the overwhelming evidence of wrong-doing not a single individual was prosecuted, let alone convicted. The Angola-Russia Debt Deal is, in short, the perfect example of how to pay a bribe in the globalised, secretive world of tax havens and, depressingly, how to get away with it.

Striking the Deal

Between 1975 and 2002, Angola was torn apart by a devastating civil war. Following Portuguese decolonisation, the country split into warring factions, the two largest of which were the MPLA and UNITA. The conflict suffered the fate of many at the time: it became a proxy in the global superpower dual of the Cold War. UNITA, headed by the notorious Jonas Savimbi, received covert aid from both the United States and apartheid South Africa. The MPLA, then a socialist organisation and the nominal government of the country, received support from both the Soviet Union and Cuba, the latter sending troops who engaged in bloody battles with UNITA fighters and pro-apartheid soldiers.

As a result of the assistance offered to the MPLA during the civil war, the Angolan government (formed by the MPLA) owed an enormous debt to Russia. By 1996, the debt had reached $5 billion. This was a significant sum for Angola whose GDP in 1996 was a meagre $7.5 billion. Angola had no way to pay the debt, while Russia could hardly have anticipated receiving the full amount.

To resolve the situation, the Angolan Minister of Economy and Finance, Augusto da Silva Tomas, issued a formal mandate - dated the 24th of April 1996 - designating Pierre Falcone and Arcadi Gaydamak as agents to negotiate with Russia on behalf of Angola. These were not your average financial intermediaries. In 1993, both Gaydamak (who was, at the time, close to Russian power players) and Falcone (himself close to the Angolan regime) had helped to arrange an enormous $790 million arms deal between Angola and Russia that became a national scandal in France (the jurisdiction where the deal was conceived and executed). In 2009, both Falcone and Gaydamak were convicted in French courts on numerous charges flowing from the weapons transaction, along with implicated French politicians. Gaydamak refused to travel to France, preferring to remain in his adopted homeland of Israel, and has never been imprisoned. Falcone served a brief time in jail. In 2011, their sentences were controversially reduced on appeal.

The exact role played by Gaydamak and Falcone in the negotiations remains murky. But by May 1996, Russia and Angola had negotiated the outline of a debt arrangement that was substantially replicated in a final agreement signed in November 1996. The terms of the final agreement were simple: Russia would reduce Angola's debt from $5 billion to $1.5 billion, which was to be paid over 15 years in 31 installments. Angola would be granted a five-year grace period, after which it was to pay Russia the stipulated amount in six monthly installments, commencing in June 2001 and ending in June 2016. Technically, Angola would be liable for interest (over and above the $1.5 billion capital amount) worth $1.39 billion, although it would seem, from the documents at our disposal, that Russia may not have ever collected the interest due.

The transaction was to be facilitated by the issuance of Promissory Notes on the part of the Angolan Central Bank. Promissory Notes are documents that commit the issuer (in this case Angola) to pay a specified amount on presentation. Angola was to provide these Promissory Notes to Russia. Each note had a face value of $48,387,096.77. Russia, meanwhile, issued a set of 31 Repayment Certificates that served as confirmation of payment. Once Angola had paid an installment to Russia, the Russian government would hand over both the Promissory Notes and the Repayment Certificates, thus extinguishing the debt.

Such a simple arrangement was not long lasting. On the 5th of March 1997, an Isle of Man company by the name of Abalone Investments entered into a contract with the Russian Ministry of Finance. Abalone – which was created purely for this transaction and was wholly owned by Arcadi Gaydamak and Pierre Falcone – agreed to purchase all of the Promissory Notes and corresponding Repayment Certificates from the Russian Ministry of Finance. Crucially, Abalone agreed to purchase the Promissory Notes from the Russian Ministry of Finance at only half their face value. Abalone would thus purchase Promissory Notes with a face value of $1.5 billion for only $750 million. The company was to buy the Notes in six 'tranches' (consisting of five or six notes) between 1997 and 2004.

Abalone was guaranteed a massive profit by means of a complementary agreement it signed with Sonangol, the Angolan state oil producer, on the 30th of May 1997. According to this agreement, Sonangol committed to purchasing the Promissory Notes from Abalone at their full face value, totalling $1.5 billion, even though Abalone had an agreement to purchase the Notes at half their face value ($750 million) from the Russian Ministry of Finance.

The entire transaction was to be managed by means of escrow agreements (one between Abalone and Russia, the other between Abalone and Sonangol) managed by the Swiss Bank Corporation (SBC) which later, by merger, became the financial giant UBS. Intriguingly, internal UBS memoranda reveal that Abalone had a powerful friend that helped convince SBC to play this role: the massive multinational oil trader Glencore, itself no stranger to controversy following the pardoning of its chief, Marc Rich, of criminal charges by President Clinton as the US leader's last official act in office. [Editor's Note: See Chapter One by Ken Silverstein for more on Glencore].

UBS documents confirm that it was Glencore that presented the arrangement to the bank and that their backing was influential in convincing SBC to become party to the agreements. Glencore, moreover, paid the initial banking fees incurred by Abalone's escrow agreements, and promised SBC that it would 'reimburse all costs and fees of third parties that could be incurred by [the escrow bank] in case of litigation relating to [the] escrow agreement.' Why Glencore was so supportive is unclear, although it is known that Sonangol was to raise the funds to pay back the debt by means of a pre-financing agreement with Glencore, which would have earned it a tidy profit.

The bigger question, however, is the simplest: why was Abalone offered the opportunity to make such an enormous profit? In later legal proceedings it was claimed that Abalone had absorbed a great deal of commercial risk by committing to buy the debt from Russia at a time when Angola's financial travails may have made such a decision questionable. Angola, meanwhile, might have argued that Abalone's involvement introduced some flexibility into the arrangement, which may have allowed Angola to pay back Abalone on a more dilatory schedule.

In reality neither outcome prevailed. In the agreements signed with the Russian Ministry of Finance, Abalone was not obliged to purchase the Promissory Notes at a certain time. Instead, the contractual arrangement with Russia constituted nothing more than a right of first refusal, for which Abalone was only required to pay an upfront fee of $4.5 million (a pittance compared to its anticipated profit). Equally friendly terms were on offer in Abalone's agreement with Sonangol, according to which, Sonangol would be forced to pay Abalone immediately on presentation of a Promissory Note. Sonangol, remarkably, could not force Abalone to sell Promissory Notes even if Sonangol approached them with the requisite funds.

Combined, these agreements meant that Abalone absorbed absolutely no commercial risk – they weren't obliged to buy Notes from Russia and if they did, they could present them to Sonangol for immediate repayment (earning a massive profit to boot). In addition, it would seem that both Russia and Angola were directly prejudiced by the agreements, raising questions as to why they bothered to include Abalone in the arrangement. On Russia's side, they would only receive half of what they anticipated, and weren't even guaranteed to get those payments, as Abalone was not obliged to buy. Angola, meanwhile, would pay double what Russia was actually willing to accept.

Moreover, one of the major attractions of the original debt agreements was that Angola could pay back Russia on an extended timeline, with a five-year grace period. But because Abalone was due to buy all the Notes from Russia by 2004, and given that Sonangol would have to pay Abalone whenever it presented a Promissory Note, Sonangol could very easily have been forced to pay back the full debt by 2004, rather than by 2016 as first anticipated.

That Russia was willing to accept such a reduced rate and that Angola could potentially have been relieved of their money on such an accelerated schedule, raises one key question: why did they not simply dispense with Abalone, and enter into more favourable terms directly? If this was done, at least one side – Angola – could have saved $750 million, while Russia would incur no further losses.

The advantages offered to Abalone – and the disadvantages

to Angola and Russia – make it difficult not to suspect some form of criminal conspiracy. The timing of the whole affair exacerbates the matter. Recall that Russia and Angola signed their original agreement in November 1996. Only a month prior, the Angolan government passed a decree allowing the Promissory Notes to be generated by the deal to be sold on the open market – paving the way for the insertion of a debt dealer like Abalone. This despite the fact that the Promissory Notes had not even been issued at that time (this would only be done in January 1997). Abalone Investments, meanwhile, was incorporated on the Isle of Man a mere 12 days after this decree was issued, and nine days before the signing of Russia and Angola's founding agreement. This suggests that the entire Debt Deal was conceived with Abalone's involvement in mind.

Paying the Angolans

With the formal agreements signed, the Debt Deal proceeded apace. Between October 1997 and July 2000, Sonangol transferred $774,193,548.32 to Abalone's UBS account in Geneva. Although matters became somewhat complicated from 1999 onwards (discussed below), Abalone appears to have purchased 16 notes from the Russian Ministry of Finance via transfers of cash and debt instruments.

Abalone distributed the profits from this period widely – and curiously. Later investigations by French and Swiss authorities revealed that large sums of money were transferred to five powerful Angolan politicians, all of whom would have overseen or could have influenced the Debt Deal as a result of their official positions. The most prominent recipient of funds was the Angolan President Jose Eduardo Dos Santos, who received $36.25 million. The second most senior was Elisio de Figueiredo, an Angolan diplomatic stalwart who has served as an ambassador since 1976. De Figueiredo received $17.557 million.

French investigations into the "Angolagate" scandal showed that both Dos Santos and de Figueiredo were paid via similar mechanisms. In October 1997, $48 million was transferred from Abalone's UBS account into an account by the name of Enirep at the Banque de Gastion Edmond De Rothschild in Luxembourg. Pierre Falcone was the beneficial owner of Enirep. In October and November 1997 money was transferred from Enirep to two further accounts: Intersul ($36.5 million) and Bracewell Management ($7.38 million). Intersul was beneficially owned by Dos Santos, while Bracewell was owned by de Figueiredo.

Oddly, in March 1998 the funds in the two accounts had to be moved quickly after Falcone's bank demanded the accounts be closed. Falcone instructed another bank – Banque Internationale a Luxembourg (BIL) to form three companies in Panama with the names of Dramal (owned by Falcone), Camparal (owned by dos Santos) and Tutoral (owned by de Figueiredo). The funds were transferred to the three accounts via another account, named Citibank NA, also held at BIL. Such are the complications of shifting funds between numerous offshore jurisdictions and tax havens.

Another recipient of funds was Joaquim Duarte da Costa David, who received $8 million in two payments from Abalone in April and July 2000. The funds were transferred into an account beneficially controlled by a company by the name of Penworth Ltd, owned by da Costa David. He would have been directly involved in the conception of the Debt Deal, as he served as Director General of Sonangol from 1989 to 1998, after which he became Minister of Finance (until 2000) and Minister of Industry (until 2010).

A second Sonangol bigwig also received funds: Jose Carlos de Castro Paiva. Paiva, in addition to being close to Dos Santos, has served as the director of Sonangol UK from 1987 to date. Exactly how Paiva was paid by Abalone is somewhat unclear. The evidence that he received funds was a bizarre Accord signed between Switzerland and Angola in 2004 that covered the transfer of funds held by Angolan officials in Switzerland (flowing from the Debt Deal) back into their hands. The funds had been frozen as a result of abortive Swiss criminal investigations. Attached to the Accord was an annex that identified the company Midas – owned by Paiva – as holding an account at Lombard, Odier, Darier & Hentsch in Geneva. As of September 2004, Midas had a balance of $4.465 million.

Jose Leitao da Costa e Silva, Minister in the Office of the Presidency from 1992 to 2004, was the final Angolan recipient of funds from Abalone, and holder of a unique distinction: he was the only official not to be paid via circuitous means. On the 6th of July 2000 a payment of $3m was made directly into the Swiss HSBC Guyerzeller bearing Silva's own name. If any transaction should have caused UBS to file a suspicious transaction report, this was it. Incidentally, in the same Accord that identified Midas as belonging to de Castro Paiva, Jose Leitao da Costa e Silva's account was stated to have a balance of $3,358,000. This raises the possibility that an additional $358,000 was transferred to Silva's account by Abalone.

Things Get Complicated

Although the mechanics of the Debt Deal were straightforward, the transaction faced a number of obstacles between 1997 and its final conclusion in 2005 that forced a number of alterations in the agreements. In 1999, Abalone was unable to purchase Promissory Notes in cash from the Russian Ministry of Finance, probably in no small part because it dissipated all profits made at an earlier stage to Angolan officials in addition to Gaydamak and Falcone.

To resolve the situation, Abalone entered into a new set of arrangements with the Ministry. Remarkably, considering how well Abalone was already doing out of the Debt Deal, the new arrangement made the deal progressively more lucrative for Abalone. According to an amendment signed in August 1999, Abalone would cease to transfer funds directly to the Russian Ministry of Finance. Instead, the company would purchase the Angolan Promissory Notes by exchanging them for Russian debt instruments (known as PRINs and IANs) that could be purchased on the open market. Abalone would transfer $1 of PRINs and IANs (with PRINs constituting the largest share) at their face value for every $1 of Angolan Promissory Notes (thus exchanging $48 million worth of PRINs at their face value while Russia would purchase one Angolan Promissory Note to the same value).

However, the PRINs and IANs were trading for a fraction of their face value on the open market. On 23 August 1999 (the date the amendment was signed), for example, $100 worth of PRINs was trading at a paltry $10.54 on the open market; IANs were trading at $14.42 for $100. Because of market fluctuations, it is possible that Abalone could have purchased $48 million face value of PRINs/IANs for as little as $5 million if they got the best deal, giving them a massive $43 million profit on each $48 million Promissory Note bought from Russia and sold to Angola. (Taking the other extreme of the market it is difficult to see how Abalone could have paid more than $17 million for each $48 million Promissory Note.) It is unclear why Russia agreed to accept PRINs/IANs from Abalone, probably knowing that it would cost Abalone a fraction of their original commitment, and given the further prejudice to the Russian position as a result.

Roughly at this time, Vitaly Malkin became a partner in the enterprise. Much like Gaydamak, Malkin was a major player on the Russian scene. In 2004, Malkin was elected to the Russian House of Parliament. He only resigned this position in 2013, and under something of a cloud: allegations swirled that he unlawfully held dual Israeli and Russian citizenship and had substantial assets in Canada. Malkin is now an extremely wealthy man after running successful banking and metallurgical companies with his partner (and current Prime Minister of Georgia), Boris Ivanishvilli. In 2008, Forbes valued his personal net wealth at around $1 billion. In 2012, Malkin's tax statements reflected an income of $33.6 million, making him the wealthiest member of Russia's Parliament.

On 20 December 1999, Malkin purchased 25 percent of Abalone directly from Arcadi Gaydamak for $60 million. Malkin thus became involved in the company at the very time it was likely to reap its largest profits (due to the adoption of the PRINs/IANs exchange mechanism). In one of the purchase agreements between Malkin and Gaydamak, Malkin was referred to as a "representative of R K Bank," which presumably refers to Rossiyskiy Kredit Bank. Malkin was the co-owner of RK Bank with Boris Ivanishvilli.

Another alteration was made in October 1999. In that month, Russia opted to terminate its Escrow Agreement with UBS, and wrote a letter asking the bank to return the Notes in its possession to Russia. This, it appears, was never done. Instead of using UBS as the Escrow Bank, Abalone was directed to transfer the PRINs/IANs to Russia's nominated bank, Sberinvest Moscow. UBS, despite the notice that it should no longer serve as escrow for the Notes, continued to receive payments from Sonangol, make payments from the Abalone account, and release Promissory Notes and Repayment Certificates to Sonangol, until July 2000.

And On to Cyprus!

In late 2000 and early 2001 the Deal faced its largest obstacle. Gaydamak and Falcone were being investigated in France for their roles in the Angolagate scandal, leading French authorities to issue warrants for their arrest. Switzerland was running its own parallel investigation and, in February 2001, accounts relating to the Deal were frozen in Geneva. The Abalone account was only unfrozen in

2004 on the orders of the Geneva courts.

For the Deal to continue the principals needed to change jurisdiction. In 2001, Gaydamak opened a new account in the name of Sberinvest at the Russian Commercial Bank, in Cyprus. Remarkably, Gaydamak undertook this change without informing Falcone or Malkin. Both would later sue Gaydamak, claiming that he had effectively cut them out of the Deal from this point onwards, allegedly relying on a dubious Abalone Power of Attorney document signed by Gaydamak's principal financial administrator, Joelle Mamane.

Between March and August 2001, Sonangol transferred $618,235,483.25 to the Sberinvest Cyprus Account. Together with their earlier transfer of funds to the Abalone Geneva account, this should have entirely extinguished Angola's debts. However, unbeknownst to Angola, Gaydamak transferred debt instruments to Russia only sufficient to purchase a portion of the Promissory Notes and Repayment Certificates from Russia.

Gaydamak actively promoted the ruse that the debt had been paid. In 2004, he wrote to Angola that all the necessary funds had been received from Angola, and that the debt to Russia had thus been settled. However, in reality, Russia had failed to receive payment for the final eight Promissory Notes still in its possession.

This swindle was only fully uncovered, belatedly, in 2005 during a meeting between Angolan and Russian officials. When Angolan officials stated that they had completely settled the debt, Russia claimed to still be owed for the eight Promissory Notes and accrued interest.

The matter was resolved, finally, in November 2005 when Angola agreed to pay the full face value of the remaining eight Notes (worth $387 million) to Russia. Gaydamak, meanwhile, was to pay back $206 million he had received from Angola but failed to pay to Russia.

It is unclear if Gaydamak ever paid the $206 million back to Angola. If he did not, then Angola would have paid $1.779 billion to settle a debt of only $1.5 billion. If he did, Angola still paid a net amount of $1.573 billion—$73 million more than had been stipulated in Angola's 1997 agreement with Abalone.

In either event, the Deal still made little sense for either country. If Angola had paid the funds directly to Russia on the same terms as Abalone was able to buy the Notes from Angola, it would have saved at least $823 million, and maybe as much as $1.029 billion:

more than 13 per cent of the country's entire GDP in 1996.

Similarly, if Russia had dealt with Angola and directly received all the funds that were paid by Angola to Abalone, it could have made an additional $750 million. In either scenario, one of the Treasuries was significantly prejudiced by the insertion of Abalone Investments into the Deal.

Turning Friends into Foes

The scandal does not end there. From the proceeds of his Cyprus adventure, an important part of which was swindled out of Angola, Gaydamak made himself a billionaire. Using his profits from the Cyprus phase of the Deal, Gaydamak invested in a series of investment funds to the value of as much as $325 million. By 2005, these investments were reportedly worth $1.25 billion. Pierre Falcone and Malkin both litigated against Gaydamak in the Israeli courts in 2008, claiming that they were due their fair share of this profit. The case was dismissed on technical grounds.

But when Gaydamak tried to cash in the funds, he was hamstrung by Luxembourg and Israeli officials, who were concerned about money laundering. As a result of a Luxembourg investigation, considerable funds belonging to Gaydamak were frozen. According to Luxembourg press reports, he was only able to have the funds released to his accounts in Cyprus in December 2005 after allegedly claiming that the funds belonged to a charitable trust called the Dorset Foundation.

To undertake the entire Cyprus operation, Gaydamak relied on the services of his confidante and financial administrator, Joelle Mamane and her husband Gad Boukobza. Mamane had also played a critical role in the earlier phase of the Debt Deal, serving as managing director of Abalone from March 1999. Unsurprisingly considering the deficit of trust and fair play that marked the entire Debt Deal, Gaydamak came to believe that he too had been swindled. As of September 2012, Gaydamak was reportedly litigating against Mamane and Boukobza in Luxembourg. Gaydamak claims that they used their fiduciary powers to steal €600 million of Gaydamak's profits from his Cyprus adventure. The court is yet to reach a verdict.

All Profit, No Loss

The sheer number of jurisdictions, ruses and revisions that marked the Debt Deal has made it hard to estimate the total profits of all the participants. But based on the documents at our disposal, they were likely to be massive – and audacious, considering how little legitimate value middlemen like Gaydamak and Falcone seemed to have offered any party. Banking documents suggest that Gaydamak was the largest earner, receiving $138 million in payments from Abalone. The second largest winner was Falcone, who received $124 million. Malkin, the late-comer, earned $48 million. Combined with the near $70 million that made it into the pockets of Angolan officials, these figures suggest that at least $386 million was made by middlemen and Angolan officials off the deal.

And that's only what we can trace so far. Between October 1997 and July 2000, Abalone made numerous transfers to companies and accounts out of its UBS Geneva account whose true beneficial owners are still a mystery. In total, just over $290 million was transferred to individuals and companies whose identities remain secret. Similarly, between March 2001 and December 2001, huge sums were transferred out of Gaydamak's Cyprus Sberinvest shell to unidentified recipients: $105 million worth. Thus, $395 million was transferred over a period of four years to unknown individuals and companies. Considering the dubious nature of the entire Deal, it is not entirely impossible that at least some of these funds made their way into the hands of politically powerful players who may have overseen the transaction.

With such enormous sums being transferred into private hands, the very least citizens of these countries could reasonably expect, and demand, is the loss of liberty of the beneficiaries and the Deal's architects. Instead, not a single participant in the Deal has ever faced criminal charges, despite the clearly dubious nature of the Deal and the reams of evidence in the public domain - which has been made available in full to prosecutors in Switzerland, while complaints have been laid in Angola.

And that is perhaps the biggest tragedy of the Angola-Russia Debt Deal: it is not just a textbook example of how to pay a bribe, it is confirmation of how easy it is to get away with it.

Andrew Feinstein is the author of *The Shadow World: Inside the Global Arms Trade*, 'the most complete account [of the arms trade] ever written' according to the Washington Post. Andrew is a former South African ANC MP, who as ranking ANC member of the Public Accounts Committee attempted to investigate the South African Arms Deal, an investigation that was neutered, leading to his resignation as an MP. Andrew is a founding director of Corruption Watch UK. A recipient of the Open Society's International Fellowship, he is also the author of *After the Party: Corruption, the ANC and South Africa's Uncertain Future* and the chapter on arms trade corruption in the *Oxford Handbook of Organised Crime* (2012).

Paul Holden is a South African-born and London-based historian, researcher, writer and activist. He has published four books to date on issues related to corruption, governance and democratic practice in South Africa. His major investigative work to date was the book *The Devil in the Detail: How the Arms Deal Changed Everything* (2011), which collated the result of years of detailed investigation into South Africa's biggest post-apartheid scandal. Since 2009, Paul has worked closely with Andrew Feinstein, acting as the lead researcher and co-author for Feinstein's *The Shadow World*.

Chapter Four

Dr. Davis Wants His Candy: "Pay to Prescribe" Bribery in Life Sciences

Kathleen Hamann

As Anti-Corruption Policy Counsel and Trial Attorney in the Fraud Section of the U.S. Department of Justice's Criminal Division over the past eight years, contributing author Kathleen Hamann knows a thing or two about corruption schemes. In this chapter, Hamann offers a glimpse of the type of work she did prosecuting the corruption of publicly-employed health care providers. And while the story in this chapter is fictitious, recent big name anti-bribery investigations of pharmaceutical companies in China proves that the risk in the life sciences industry for this kind of improper activity is all too real.

Hugh, the Regional Sales Director for PharmaCo, sighed as he read the email. He knew it was coming. It was from Dimitri, head of TransMedSlobovia, PharmaCo's distributor in Slobovia. It was a single sentence:

"Dr. Davis wants his candy. We're overdue."

Hugh knew that their chief competitor had been courting Dr. Davis for months, and that they offered better "candy." While he had arranged trips all over the world for Dr. Davis and his wife, ostensibly for conferences Davis never actually attended, and even lavished him with World Cup tickets, expensive meals, and donated to the charity he headed, their competition had offered him straight cash. His competitor had Godiva, and all Hugh was offering were M&M's.

Dr. Davis was one of the largest prescribers of PharmaCo's products, not only in Slobovia, but worldwide. Dimitri once joked that Davis sold so much of PharmCo's product that he was probably making all of his patients take it whether they needed it or not. Moreover, he was a key opinion leader. In addition to his own practice, he was regularly consulted by the Slobovian government on licensing new products, and was on the tender committee at University Hospital, the capital's largest medical center. Slobovia had an all-public health care system, which meant payments came late and sales were hard to predict. PharmaCo was barely squeaking out a profit this quarter as it was, and Hugh could hardly afford to have Davis switch companies.

As Hugh saw his annual bonus going up in smoke, he considered his options. When he had set up the contract with TransMedSlobovia, Dimitri had mentioned his "other" company, MarketMedSlobovia, which did "marketing surveys." Hugh had signed a second contract with MarketMedSlobovia, which was paid a percentage of TransMedSlobovia's sales in advance each quarter. MarketMedSlobovia was registered in the Isle of Man and was paid in Cyprus, but no one had ever noticed that when he registered MarketMedSlobovia as one of PharmaCo's vendors. MarketMedSlobovia simply sent an invoice each quarter listing amorphous "market advice" that they had never provided, which Hugh knew was used as a slush fund to keep the doctors happy. When PharmaCo's Compliance team asked Hugh about doing due diligence on the two companies, Hugh told them that their intermediaries in Slobovia had been working with the company for 20 years without trouble, so they were a low priority for review. Noting that Slobovia had a reasonable Corruption Perception Index score, Compliance agreed that Dimitri's companies were "low risk" and left MarketMedSlobovia and TransMedSlobovia alone, never even noticing they were both owned by the same person. So while Hugh knew that the money was at least available, he still had to find a way to get cash to the doctors without it showing up on any of PharmaCo's books and records.

PharmaCo did have that clinical study going on in a neighboring country, Hugh thought, maybe they could sign a civil contract with Dr. Davis and pay him for consulting on the study? He would have to make the amount they paid Davis – which was $20 every time he prescribed one of PharmaCo's products – match up to some kind of hourly rate. That would be complicated, though, making up different hours every quarter so that it somehow matched what Davis was owed. Hugh discarded the idea.

He could say the payments were a fee for managing patients in the study – a per patient fee. That would work, as they would just call each prescription a patient in the study. They would have to backdate the contract, of course. But then he realized that they would have to register the patients with the study, as well as Dr. Davis' participation, and that would not work because the study was in another country. He scrapped the idea of the clinical study.

He had another thought. MarketSlobovia could create a conference and just fake hotel invoices and agendas for an in-country training session. If it was in-country, Hugh could probably slide it by those eagle eyes in Compliance. It would all be documented, of course, and Compliance would never check to see if the conference ever occurred. He could pay MarketMedSlobovia for it, stick it into the medical education budget and it would have no impact on his marketing budget or sales figures. Davis would get his candy.

Hugh just had to convince the Director of Medical Education to pay for it. That would probably work for the short term problem, but it would not help with the longer term issue of paying Davis' new, higher rate – the Director of Medical Education would get suspicious eventually. He emailed Dimitri back from his personal email, describing his temporary solution, and asked for suggestions for a longer-term solution. "Don't respond to my PharmaCo address," Hugh added, "we need to keep this off company email."

Two days later, Dimitri emailed back with a solution. University Hospital has an affiliated foundation for doctor training, Dimitri explained, but there was no oversight. Dr. Davis and three other doctors at the hospital, all department heads, decided how the money would be spent, without audits or bookkeepers. Dimitri explained the elegance of the solution. PharmaCo could include donations to the foundation in their bid for the tenders, which would allow him to negotiate the bribe at the same time they negotiated the contract, and Dr. Davis could dole out the cash to the rest of the department heads to keep their sales high. Donations like that were not uncommon, and if it was part of the bid, Hugh wouldn't even have to get approval from PharmaCo for a charitable donation.

Hugh liked the idea, but worried about the impact it would have on his budget. His profit numbers would get even worse. Dimitri had a solution for that too. They would build the cost of the "donation" into the price. Then Hugh would file an "addendum" with PharmaCo, either dropping the price back to the normal level or giving University Hospital a rebate, but the addendum would never go to the hospital. Dimitri would take the money from the higher prices and donate it to the foundation. Brilliant!

There was just one problem. How could Dr. Davis justify the awarding of the contract to PharmaCo at substantially higher market prices? Dimitri had a solution for that too. Dr. Davis would limit the bidding options, either by drafting the tender so that only PharmaCo's products would qualify or would only invite a few companies to bid, and TransMedSlobovia and MarketMedSlobovia would be the other bidders. They would put in substantially higher bids than PharmaCo and would exclude donations, making PharmaCo's price look reasonable. Pharmaceuticals were already twice as expensive in Slobovia than anywhere else in the region, so it should go off without a hitch.

With the problem solved, Hugh made a note to himself – "Talk to Finance about acquiring TransMedSlobovia and make it a subsidiary." Now that the system was set up, might as well bring it in-house.

*   *   *

Bribery of publicly-employed health care providers is not the traditional Foreign Corrupt Practices Act (FCPA) violation that everyone was familiar with ten years ago. It is not briefcases full of cash in exchange for huge government contracts. It is usually small amounts – a hundred dollars here, a thousand dollars there. That makes it no less harmful. In many ways, bribery in health care systems is the most directly damaging of any industry – every dollar that goes into a bribe is a dollar that does not go into providing care. All of those small payments add up to millions and millions of dollars, which are surgeries not performed, life-saving drugs not received, and care not provided.

According to U.K. authorities, bribery has saturated the orthopedic market in Greece to such an extent that the cost of a replacement knee has been between two and four times the European average. Bribery in life sciences has been the focus of prosecutions in the United States, Germany, Italy, Poland, Greece, the United Kingdom, and elsewhere, including industry-wide sweeps, and investigations into pharmaceutical companies by Chinese authorities have also recently made the news. Prosecutors in Poland, who have recently conducted a number of prosecutions of bribery in the medical device industry, have said that as much as fifteen percent of Poland's annual spending in orthopedics was being lost to bribery before their investigations began. According to Transparency International, the United Kingdom's National Health Service's (NHS) anti-fraud unit reports that it has stopped corruption totaling more than $300 million, leading to losses to NHS of $1.2 billion – enough to build 10 new hospitals. Payments to "foundations" with no oversight, where the doctors could spend the money on anything they wanted, were once common in Canada. An ombudsman's report in Australia identified a doctor who was performing unnecessary surgeries to keep his bribe rates high. This is not just a problem in the most corrupt of countries - it happens everywhere.

While Dr. Davis, Hugh, and Dimitri are fictional characters, all of the scenarios described above are actual schemes used to pay bribes in the medical device and pharmaceutical industries. Over time, the schemes have grown more sophisticated and harder to detect. The days of openly providing lavish travel and entertainment to doctors are long over, but that just means that the bribery has been driven underground. It hasn't gone away. As the schemes shift, corporate compliance has to adapt to keep up.

There are three main areas where bribery in life sciences occurs. The first is at the regulatory stage – when a company is seeking approval of a new product. These bribes more closely resemble the more familiar payments in the FCPA world – a large payment to a regulator in order to bring something to market. Because of the involvement of higher-level people and the difficulty in hiding larger payments, it is easier to identify these situations and build protections to stop them.

The second is tendering and listing – the process that makes an approved product actually available, whether it is listing for reimbursement, winning a hospital tender, or related activities. These bribes go to hospital administrators, physicians preparing the tender specifications, provincial health care officials, tender committees, and so forth. These are harder for the business community to protect against, particularly in countries where every hospital runs its own tenders and where there may be hundreds in a given country in a single year.

The third is payments to physicians and other hospital staff, such as nurses, themselves – so-called "pay to prescribe" bribes, like those described above. These are the most invidious. Bribes in those cases often come from the lowest level – the sales people out in the hinterlands every day. Distributors and acquisitions pose the greatest risks for the industry. All distributors and newly-acquired subsidiaries should undergo due diligence – both legal and financial - and their profit margins should be benchmarked, regardless of how long-standing the relationship is, and risks need to be assessed on an industry-specific basis, not on general tools like the Corruption Perceptions Index. Acquisitions cannot be run by local staff untrained in anti-bribery issues or lacking specific expertise in identifying red flags and problem areas.

Of course, not all of the red flags described above are specific to life sciences. Third-country intermediaries and off-shore payments should always bring heightened scrutiny. Multiple contracts with affiliated entities should have a specific business purpose, justifying not only why there is a need to retain multiple companies, particularly if they are owned by the same person or people but also why there is a specific need for multiple contracts. Amendments or addenda to sales contracts should be rare and specifically justified, and confirmed by the contracting entity where possible.

Other issues are industry-specific. Medical and professional education needs to be separated from sales and marketing to the maximum degree possible, to ensure that education and training are not being used as bribe conduits. Contracts with health care providers, whether for clinical trials, training, or other consultation services, should always be signed in advance and be carefully scrutinized to ensure that services are actually being performed and that payment rates make sense for the type of contract signed.

Industry codes in life sciences have come a long way, and resources are available for small and large companies alike. Robust policies on booth fees, conferences, gifts, hospitality, and travel are also needed, and should include spot-checking all the way down to the vendor level (such as calling the hotel to ensure the conference occurred). Periodic audits in high-risk countries that are prone to FCPA risks are also critical in an industry that is so far flung. "Foundations" that are affiliated with hospitals and other medical institutions should be scrutinized to ensure there is adequate oversight and, wherever possible, providing in-kind donations is preferable to giving cash. Most importantly, in life sciences, periodic risk assessments and regular adjustments to compliance and audit procedures are needed to keep up with the new schemes as they develop.

Paying doctors to use the right product is a cost that no company should bear, but companies in some countries have gotten into "bribe wars" over physicians who are key opinion leaders. Each tries to outbribe the other. Once the bribes start, they only get bigger – higher payments, more doctors, ever-increasing demands. Bribery also carries huge reputational risk, particularly in the health care industry. No company wants its hard-won reputation tarnished by rumors that its products were prescribed not because they were the best (or perhaps when they were not even needed), but because doctors were paid to do it. Reducing bribery in the industry not only takes the costs of the bribes out of the bottom line, it eventually increases sales as countries more efficiently use their health care budgets to provide more care – four knees sold in Greece instead of one.

A great deal of creativity has gone into developing the schemes to pay bribes in the life sciences, and those schemes will continue to evolve. The best resistance is a corporate culture that promotes sales not for their own sake, but because of the benefits the products provide, and where compliance is prioritized. It is not only healthier for the patient, it results in healthier public care systems, and healthier and stronger companies.

Kathleen Hamann is a partner at White & Case LLP, specializing in anticorruption, transnational and extraterritorial criminal law. She previously was the longest-tenured prosecutor in the FCPA Unit of the Department of Justice, where she oversaw the industry-wide investigation into bribery in the medical device and pharmaceutical industries. Prior to that, Ms. Hamann was a Foreign Service Officer at the Department of State for more than ten years, focusing on anticorruption and transnational law enforcement cooperation.

Chapter Five

From Offsets to Jumbo Jets: Corruption in the Arms Trade

Barnaby Pace

When signed in 1985 between the United Kingdom and Saudi Arabia, Al-Yamamah, which means "the dove" in Arabic, was Britain's largest arms deal in history. Over the course of the next twenty years, it netted the British government an impressive $80 billion. But reports eventually emerged that the deal involved massive kickbacks to Saudi officials, most of which were paid by BAE Systems, formerly British Aerospace. Those revelations would help build momentum for passage of the ground-breaking UK Bribery Act in 2010. This chapter explores the features of the deal and explains how Al-Yamamah serves as a wider example for how the arms trade can be susceptible to corruption.

The arms trade has been rife with corruption historically. One study by Transparency International, based on information from official sources and intelligence agencies around the world, estimated that 40% of corruption in global trade occurs in the arms industry.[1]

While many companies have recognized that they're in the enforcement crosshairs, allegations of corrupt arms companies are not thin on the ground. Few rival the scale and the scope

---

[1] This figure was calculated in 2003 by Joe Roeber in work undertaken for Transparency International. Roeber, J., *Hard-wired for corruption: the arms trade and corruption*, Prospect, no. 113, (28 Aug. 2005).

of evidence cast against BAE Systems ("BAE"). BAE holds the distinction of having been the prime contractor for what may have been the single most pervasively corrupt contract of all time, the Al Yamamah arms deal between the UK government and the Saudi Arabian governments, which has continued for over two decades after beginning in 1985. The deal was worth over £43 billion[2] in which, according to police estimates, over £6 billion were made in illicit payments.[3] BAE did not always act alone, working at times in partnership with other arms firms and hand in glove with governments. As Vince Cable, currently Business Minister in the UK put it, "the British government was up to its neck in this whole business. Government ministers were almost certainly fully aware of what was happening."[4] One agent told reporters, with awe in his voice, "I've worked for a lot of aircraft companies, but BAE is the only one with such an institutionalized system."[5]

It is at times surprising that BAE got caught at all. It took years of investigation by reporters, members of parliament and civil society campaigners to reveal what is likely only a fraction of BAE's total exploits. In the end, BAE reached settlements with authorities in the UK and the US, which cost the company around $480 million. But other reports indicate that the true scale of BAE's activities was never fully examined by the authorities because of either lack of political backing or insufficient legal tools necessary to effectively prosecute the company.

Even so, the Al Yamamah arms deal has had far-reaching consequences:

- The investigation into BAE resulted in episodes of white-washing within the UK Government, including Tony Blair's eventual personal intervention in the case, damaging overall

---

[2] *BAE cashes in on £40bn Arab jet deal,* Sunday Times, 20 August 2006.
[3] *Secrets of Al Yamamah,* Guardian, 'The BAE Files', *available at* http://www.theguardian.com/baefiles/page/0,,2095831,00.html.
[4] Leigh and Evans, *BAE admits guilt over corrupt arms deals,* Guardian, 6 February 2010.
[5] Leigh and Evans, *BAE accused of hiding cash,* Guardian, 5 December 2003.

public perception of British rule of law;[6]
- The deal further tarnished the reputation of the Saudi regime, underscoring the grand lifestyle of its royal family;
- On a more positive note, the deal became a turning point in the public's understanding of corruption and influenced the passage of the 2010 UK Bribery Act.

It is useful to use the Al Yamamah arms deal to understand how bribes are paid and how corruption can be more successfully investigated, prosecuted and prevented in the future.

How to Bribe a Saudi Prince

Dick Evans, the former BAE Chairman, was said to have won the Al Yamamah deal, the largest arms deal in British history, because of his ability to swallow sheep's eyeballs as though they were cocktail canapés at banquets.[7] The ability to consume unusual food while keeping up the arms dealer schmoozing routine may have had its part, but really BAE and the UK government secured business in Saudi Arabia by understanding the nature of the regime there and how "the system" works.

A red flag in arms deals in Saudi Arabia, as well as many other countries, is that of the redundant "fixer," the intermediary between a foreign company and the buyer with no clear purpose. (Fixers, in this case, can be distinguished from legitimate commercial intermediaries with a well-defined and legitimate role.) Such a fixer may be brought in even if the foreign company is already on site and has strong contacts in the government. The fixer's job may include help bridging the cultural divide between the foreign business and the Saudis, but in the worst cases, he will find inappropriate ways to influence the decisions of the government to favor their client over their competitors.

Each fixer, in order to carry out their role, will have a "sponsor," usually a prince. The fixer and the prince may share the profits of any commission between themselves and any other figures that

---

[6] *Documents reveal that Blair urged end to BAE-Saudi corruption investigation,* Corner House, *available at* http://www.thecornerhouse.org.uk/resource/documents-reveal-blair-urged-end-bae-saudi-corruption-investigation.
[7] Macalister, *Profile: Sir Dick Evans, BAE chairman,* Guardian, 5 February 2010.

might have to be appeased such as officials, military officers or other princes.

Smart fixers ally themselves with the most powerful sponsors possible, those who know what contracts are to be awarded and who can best influence the decision-making process. The fixer's role is to find a company looking for contracts that his sponsor can influence, negotiating a price that will produce the greatest profit for the fixer and sponsor. In order to attract clients, a fixer relies on his reputation for being influential and on the real power of his sponsor.

In the case of the Al Yamamah arms deal, the fixer was Wafic Said. Said is a Syrian-Saudi businessman who had close links to Prince Sultan, the then-Saudi Defense minister. He also had close contacts with the UK Conservative party, to which he donated at least £350,000 during the Thatcher premiership. It has even been alleged that Said employed Mark Thatcher, the son of Margaret Thatcher, to act as a back channel to the former prime minister.[8]

Adnan Khashoggi, the man who became infamous in the 1970s for negotiating arms deals on behalf of international companies operating in Saudi Arabia, succeeded largely because of the mystique that he wove around himself, claiming to be the richest man in the world at one time.[9] This is of course a highly dangerous game; there are many fixers who will attempt to scam companies by claiming to be more influential than they really are. Others may work with multiple competitors for the same deal, misrepresenting the scale of the bribes needed and then keeping a larger portion to maximize their own profit.

There is a further complicating factor: the "skimmer." The skimmer is a more senior decision maker, often the final decision maker on the deal, the person whose demands must therefore be met to gain the contract. The skimmer is most often a senior prince, possibly in the cabinet or the head of a ministry, a province emir, head of a branch of the armed forces or the head of a royal commission in charge of a certain project or development scheme. The skimmer, the corrupt decision maker for the contract, is often in the position where all fixers and sponsors must appease him and

---

[8] Leigh & Evans, *Wafic Said*, Guardian, 7 June 2007; James, *In the public interest*, pp. 62 and 106-7; Sunday Times, 9 October 1994; Gary Murray, *Enemies of the State*, London: Simon and Schuster, 1993.
[9] Dunne, *Khashoggi's Fall*, Vanity Fair, September 1989.

compete to offer the largest bribe.

The best example of a skimmer was Prince Sultan, who as Minister for Defense and Aviation for almost fifty years as well Crown Prince, has had a huge budget at his control, the opportunity presented by an already secretive arms trade and enough power that even Kings have rarely gone against him. As both policy maker and beneficiary, Prince Sultan decides what the country needs and how the budget is to be divided and awards the contracts himself. He was certainly the main decision maker in the Al Yamamah arms deal and, as one British Ambassador concluded, "had a corrupt interest in all contracts."[10]

How to Hide Corrupt Payments in the Arms Trade

Corrupt transactions can come in forms as diverse as the different things people value. Even so, there are trends. Bribery is of course the most straightforward form of corruption. The payment can be made in any number of currencies or goods: offshore centers might be used to hide payments and indeed shield them from tax, BVI shell companies can be used and major institutions are often implicated.

The Al Yamamah arms deal featured over a billion pounds paid in quarterly payments of £30 million from a UK Government account at the Bank of England. The payments were authorised by the UK Government arms export promotion department to a Saudi Government account used by Prince Bandar, son of the then Saudi Defense Minister at the iconic Riggs Bank in Washington. The payments were sourced from a 2% commission taken by the Defense Export Service Organization (DESO), the UK arms export agency, into its Bank of England joint account with BAE on the income from the oil sales that the Saudis used to pay for the deal.[11] Overcharging, apparently with UK government knowledge, also generated funds for secret payments. The cost of Tornado jets,

---

[10] *Crown Prince Sultan Ibn Abdul-Aziz al Saud*, Telegraph, 23 October 2011, available at http://www.telegraph.co.uk/news/obituaries/politics-obituaries/8844666/Crown-Prince-Sultan-Ibn-Abdul-Aziz-al-Saud.html; David Pallister, *The arms deal they called the dove: how Britain grasped the biggest prize*, The Guardian, 15 December 2006.

[11] *Supra*, note 3; *see also* Leigh and Evans, *Attorney general responds to Bandar, £1bn and BAE*, Guardian, 8 June 2007.

the most expensive equipment bought in the Al Yamamah deal, was inflated by up to 32% with the apparent knowledge of the UK government.[12]

While there are many complex ways to hide the flow of money, one of the most difficult to trace is still cash. BAE's European agent, Count Alfons Mensdorff-Pouilly was accused by witnesses at his trial of receiving envelopes stuffed with cash.[13] It is a lesson drug dealers learned many years ago: if you can get hold of cash reasonably anonymously in the first place, then there will be no record of where that cash has gone. In the illicit arms trade, the tricky part is the quantity required, especially for large deals.

While many agents, even in the arms trade, are legitimate intermediaries, bribery schemes typically involve criminally-minded agents who go to great lengths to conceal illegal payments. In 1995, BAE had over 700 agency agreements, and it was paying at least £50 million per year to its 300+ agents.[14] A board level committee approved agency agreements.[15] Again, while many of these may have been legitimate, documents indicate that BAE developed a system of open and covert agency agreements that it used to build a system for secret payments. It built its system over years, hiding its activities through "money laundries" in offshore financial centers, in Swiss vaults,[16] through obscure offset arrangements and sometimes even through the UK government itself.

One such offshore company created by BAE was called Red Diamond, located in the British Virgin Islands. Red Diamond, at

---

[12] David Pallister, *The arms deal they called the dove: how Britain grasped the biggest prize,* The Guardian, 15 December 2006.

[13] Frederika Whitehead, *BAE faces demand to answer 'bribery' claims in Austrian court,* Exaro, 24 January 2013, available at http://www.exaronews.com/articles/4814/bae-faces-demand-to-answer-bribery-claims-in-austrian-court.

[14] G. Murphy, British Serious Fraud Office, Affidavit submitted as Annexure JDP-SW 12 in the High Court of South Africa (Transvaal Provincial Division) in the matter of Ex Parte the National Director of Public Prosecutions (applicant) re: an application for issue of search warrants in terms of Section 29(5) and 29(6) of the National Prosecuting Authority Act, No.32 of 1998, as amended (2008).

[15] *BAE's secret money machine,* Guardian, 'The BAE Files', *available at* http://www.theguardian.com/baefiles/page/0,,2095840,00.html.

[16] *Id.*

the specific direction of BAE's senior management, made 1,000 payments to agents between 1998 and 2007.[17] During that time, Red Diamond was never mentioned in any BAE accounts and to this day has never been properly explained by BAE.[18] The SFO has expressed its belief that Red Diamond was created "to ensure that corrupt payments could be made and that it would be more difficult for law enforcement agencies to penetrate the system [of covert payments]."[19]

In all, BAE developed a complex system of overt and covert agent agreements, where at least two contracts would be held, one with a modest retainer that they could admit to, and a second secret contract that promised much greater sums.[20] In order to further conceal illegality, BAE would arrange to keep the documents outside of the UK's jurisdiction. One source told Guardian reporters that they had to fly to Switzerland in the 1980s to sign secret deals on arms contracts to India.[21] BAE used a system where only a single copy of the signed agent agreements would be kept in a lawyer's vault in Switzerland and it could only be viewed in the presence of both parties.[22] In 2002, BAE drove the contents of its filing cabinets and safe containing its paperwork concerning its agents from the UK to a discreetly rented high security office in Geneva which had been swept for bugs by a trusted UK specialist.[23] The Serious Fraud Office would later conclude, "The whole system is maintained in such conditions of secrecy that there is a legitimate suspicion concerning the real purpose of the payments."[24]

---

[17] *Proposed Charging Letter from U.S. Department to State to BAE Systems, May 2011,* Campaign Against Arms Trade, *available at* http://www.caat. org.uk/resources/companies/bae-systems/BAES-Proposed-charging-letter.pdf.

[18] *Supra,* note 15.

[19] *Supra,* note 14.

[20] *Proposed Charging Letter from U.S. Department to State to BAE Systems, May 2011,* Campaign Against Arms Trade, *available at* http://www.caat. org.uk/resources/companies/bae-systems/BAES-Proposed-charging-letter.pdf; Leigh and Evans, *BAE accused of hiding cash paid to win deals,* Guardian, 5 December 2003.

[21] Leigh and Evans, *BAE accused of hiding cash paid to win deals,* Guardian, 5 December 2003.

[22] *Id.*

[23] *Id.*

[24] *Supra,* note 15.

Gifts

Although in some places gifts are a customary part of doing business, the scale of a 'gift,' ranging from items like tickets to a popular international sports event, an expensive watch, a holiday, a car or even a house, gives rise to serious concerns.

The range of gifts on one deal is again exemplified by the Al Yamamah deal. John Porter, a low level official in the UK Government arms export department on the Saudi Arabian project, was given free holidays and theater trips by BAE.[25] Saudi pilots and the Head of the Saudi Air Force had their every desire answered, including prostitutes, a house for a prince's mistress and shopping excursions so lavish that they required the chartering of airliners to carry the purchases home.[26] At the far end of the spectrum, Prince Bandar, as well as receiving at least £1 billion in payments, was given by BAE for his birthday a wide-body airbus 340 worth £75 million. The Prince claims that this aircraft is in fact property of the state, a small distinction in an absolute monarchy like Saudi Arabia, but even then few official aircraft are painted in the colors of the official's favourite American football team: in Bandar's case, the Dallas Cowboys.[27] Even BAE executives were accused of being in on the act. Former BAE Chairman Dick Evans was accused of receiving two penthouse flats worth £6 million in a complex arrangement from agents involved in the Al Yamamah arms deal.[28]

The Revolving Door

The revolving door, or post-employment of officials, is very difficult to catch and in many cases is not actually illegal, but a simple way to induce corrupt decision making. An explicit offer is not even required. Officials are less likely to be critical or make

---

[25] Leigh & Evans, *MoD official took BAE gifts,* Guardian, 6 April 2004.

[26] Michael Robinson, *BBC lifts the lid on secret BAE slush fund,* BBC News, 5 October 2004.

[27] Bandar continues to argue that this is property of the state and not his personal property. Leigh & Evans, *BAE bought £75m Airbus for Saudi prince,* Guardian, 15 June 2007.

[28] *Arms chief in cover-up over £6m penthouses,* Sunday Times, 3 February 2013, available at http://www.thesundaytimes.co.uk/sto/news/insight/article1206718.ece.

choices disadvantageous to a company that they think might employ them in the future. The employment might not even be that of the decision maker, but instead a member of their family. The scale of the problem is made clear by the number of government officials and military officers who leave office to go work for arms companies. Research by The Guardian found that in the UK, senior military officers and Ministry of Defense officials received approval for 3,572 jobs in arms companies between 1996 and 2012.[29] In the US, eighty percent of generals retiring from 2004 to 2008 took jobs with defense contractors, often while still advising the Pentagon, according to a 2010 Boston Globe investigation.[30]

One striking example of this revolving door is the experience of Sir Sherard Cowper-Coles. As Britain's Ambassador to Saudi Arabia, Cowper-Coles pressured the Serious Fraud Office to drop its investigation into the BAE-Saudi arms deals. When he left the Foreign Office, he was given a job as international business development director for BAE, focusing on the Middle East and south-east Asia.[31] There is no allegation of corruption in this case, but the danger of the official's decision-making being biased is all too real and the appearance of impropriety is unavoidable even if the parties have acted scrupulously.

Subcontractors

The arms industry, like most, has become globalized. Components for a single weapon may be sourced from all over the world, which poses problems for governments who worry about the security of their supply chain. The Pentagon, for example, estimated that seventy per cent of an estimated one million suspect parts in their equipment came from China.[32] But to the person who wishes to profit from bribery, subcontracting offers an ideal opportunity to extort bribes.

---

[29] Hopkins, Evans & Norton-Taylor, *MoD staff and thousands of military officers join arms firms*, Guardian, 15 October 2012.
[30] Bender, *From the Pentagon to the private sector*, Boston Globe, 26 December 2010.
[31] Tim Webb, *BAE Systems hires Britain's former envoy to Saudi Arabia*, 18 February 2011.
[32] *China fake parts 'used in US military equipment'*, BBC News, 22 May 2012, available at http://www.bbc.co.uk/news/world-us-canada-18155293.

On a typical major arms deal, a prime contractor wins a contract for aircraft, their facilities, support equipment, training, spare parts and other services for years to come. Each of these contracts can have layers of bribery built in.

For example take a $1 billion project paid for by the government and subject to commissions. The main contractor may agree to a 10 per cent commission equal to $100 million. But on top of that, subcontractors handling $500 million worth of the work may pay another 10 per cent commission, worth another $50 million. The suppliers of materials and equipment, whose business may be worth, say, $250 million, pay another 10 per cent commission, worth $25 million. So the total amount of commissions paid is equal to $175 million, 17.5%, not just the 10% agreed to by the top-level contractor. Given the many layers of subcontractors involved in any large contract, the quantity of bribes can escalate quickly.

On the Al Yamamah deal, Thorn EMI disclosed that it had paid £40m in commissions, 26% of their contract, for bomb fuses on the deal. A former executive for Royal Ordnance testified in court that commissions were also paid on the supply of the bombs. Rolls Royce, in turn, disclosed that it had paid £23 million as an 8% commission to an anonymous Panama entity, controlled by members of the Ibrahim family, the favoured in-laws of King Fahd. The Ibrahims had sued for a 15% commission until the issue was settled out of court.[33] Finally, Vosper Thorneycroft, another subcontractor, was also alleged to have paid a commission on its Al Yamamah contract.[34]

Offsets

Under many trade agreements and in most industries, offsets are illegal. The World Trade Organization (WTO), the North American Free Trade Agreement (NAFTA) and the European Union (EU) ban their use. However, both WTO and EU rules make an exception for the arms trade. Offsets are an economic tool through which the selling company or country promises to invest a substantial amount of money in the buying country. Sometimes,

---

[33] Evans and Leigh, *Sub-contractor's Corruption,* Guardian, 7 June 2007.
[34] Hansard, 24 January 1996, Column 455, *available at* http://www. publications.parliament.uk/pa/cm199596/cmhansrd/vo960124/ debtext/60124-51.htm.

offsets can equal as much as 150% of the contract, significantly changing the outcome of a bidding process. The offsets may be direct, taking the form of investment in businesses related to the contract, or indirect, completely unrelated to the business at hand. These agreements are also often kept secret, and they rarely live up to their promises of jobs and economic benefits to the host country. Indeed, in many cases the penalties are so small for not fulfilling offset agreements that reneging on them is often the cheaper option.

The obscurity and complexity of offset agreements pose a real corruption risk. There is little to stop the offset money either not materializing or flowing to businesses connected to decision makers. Indeed this was alleged in the South African BAE Systems case. There, the South African government was interested in buying fighter jets to modernize its defense forces. Allegedly, Defense Minister Joe Modise altered the procurement criteria to suit BAE's bid, and BAE and their partner SAAB were then given an opportunity to improve their bid by using offsets, something their competitors were not offered.[35] In the end, BAE submitted a package roughly ten times larger than any of their competitors. When the offset proposals were later evaluated by the South African Department of Trade and Industry, their value was found to have been 'grossly inflated' from $245 million to $1.6 billion.[36]

Why the Arms Trade?

There are inextricable aspects of the arms trade that make it more prone to corruption. One main feature of the arms trade is the wall of secrecy related to legitimate national security interests and commercial confidentiality which can be used to conceal conflicts of interest and corruption. As a result, the arms trade is rarely audited or held accountable. The National Audit report into the Al Yamamah arms deal between the UK and Saudi Arabia, for example, was considered so sensitive that only ten copies were kept under top security.[37] When the UK's Serious Fraud Office was denied access to the report, the SFO even considered raiding

---

[35] *Strategic Defence Packages: Joint Report,* 2001, Chapter 4, para. 4.51.10, *available at* www.info.gov.za.
[36] *Id.* at paras 4.5.3.6 & 4.5.5.3.
[37] Hansard, HC Deb, 13 February 2002, c402W.

government departments to try to gain access.[38]

A second feature is the significant financial rewards of the arms trade coupled with these low levels of accountability. Of 502 recorded violations of UN arms embargoes, only two cases have resulted in any legal accountability, and only one resulted in a prosecution.[39] In the BAE case, the company was fined around $400 million dollars by the UK and US authorities in 2010, pleading guilty to false statements and accounting practices violations. However, only a few days later, an unexpected pension windfall worth $410 million effectively cancelled out the cost of the fine.[40] The sophistication, fragmentation and in many cases opacity of global production together with the high level of technical knowledge required to understand an arms deal are further factors.

In the case of BAE, the UK investigation petered out into a charge of accounting irregularities for the company's payments to its Tanzanian agent, with the SFO and BAE both claiming that the payments were only for lobbying and technical advice, something even the judge seemed not to believe.[41] BAE's outside auditing firm, KPMG, was accused of facilitating the creation of BAE's corrupt system and ignoring audit risks. The firm eventually had the case dropped in 2013, however, due to the complexity of the activities which stretched back over decades.[42]

As we learn more about the BAE scandal and other similar corrupt schemes, we also gain better understanding of how these various types of corrupt activities can be prevented in future deals.

---

[38] Hope & Oborne, *The auditor general and Saudi arms deals,* The Spectator, 17 October 2007.

[39] Andrew Feinstein, *Shadow World: Inside the Global Arms Trade,* p.xxix, London: Penguin Books, 2012.

[40] Tom McGhie & Jenny Little, *BAE pension windfall wipes out £285m fine,* Daily Mail, 13 February 2010.

[41] *Judge flays BAE plea deal,* Corner House, 21 December 2010, *available at* http://www.thecornerhouse.org.uk/resource/judge-flays-bae-plea-deal.

[42] Adam Jones, *Watchdog drops probe into KPMG's audit of BAE,* Financial Times, 1 August 2013.

Barnaby Pace is a writer and investigator on corruption and conflict issues. He was the primary researcher for *Shadow World: Inside the Global Arms Trade*, co-author of "Sins of Commission," the lead chapter for the *SIPRI Yearbook 2011* and has worked for a range of NGOs and media outlets. He is a member of the steering committees of the UK based Campaign Against Arms Trade and Forceswatch. He has appeared as a commentator on *Sky News, BBC, Al Jazeera* and *Russia Today*. He also tweets @pace_nik and blogs at armouersfaith.wordpress.com.

Chapter Six

Bribery in China:
Many Tools in the Toolbox

Amy L. Sommers

In our 2012 edition of "How to Pay a Bribe," Amy Sommers tackled Chinese corruption in the travel services sector. Over the past year, we've witnessed an uptick in Chinese enforcement actions against foreign multinational companies, including the detainment of several foreign employees. At issue again is the worrisome use of travel agencies to mask improper payments, with GlaxoSmithKline purportedly using over 700 travel agencies to disguise bribes to Chinese government officials. In this chapter, Sommers revisits the use of travel agencies to engage in corruption in China, and also provides a few other methods that Chinese officials have been known to extort money from businesses, each more imaginative than the last.

A frequent criticism of the Chinese educational system is that it stifles creativity. The adaptability of the hydra-headed monster that is bribery in China indicates however, that the concern may not be well-founded. When confronted with new and tighter restrictions or heightened oversight, ingenuity has ensured that bribe-givers and bribe-takers have found ways to connect.

What are some of the frequent or especially clever schemes that are used? Below are just a few ways in which Chinese 'creativity' has been used to circumvent governance controls and achieve improper ends. Of course, the key to the success of any business endeavor in China is scalability. So, we must also ask what 'scalable' schemes are being used as conduits for improper benefits?

Travel Agencies

The ways travel agencies can be used to facilitate bribes in China are manifold. In the news coverage of PRC enforcement against UK-headquartered pharmaceutical company GlaxoSmithKlein, much attention has focused on the use of travel agencies to subvert GSK's compliance program. To review our explanation offered in the 2012 edition of *How to Pay a Bribe*, travel agents are used to facilitate improper benefits in the following ways:

Type of Event:	Example:
Fake Events	Conferences that are fabricated as a means of generating a pool of cash to be used for paying bribes to officials so that they would approve purchase orders for state-owned medical facilities.
Real Events with Fake Attendees	The event (e.g., a conference at a scenic tourist site) might be real, but the actual attendees would differ from those named in the approval sheets. In this way, employees could overcome the problem of doctors having already received the maximum allowable company hospitality; or attest to more invitees having attended the event than in fact attended, allowing the "surplus" to be retained by the agency for use by the sales team as a slush fund for future bribes.
Real Events with Disguised Activities	To evade restrictions against lavish entertainment, sales team members have the travel agent bill the company for approved activities, such as a bus tour for a large group, when in reality, golf at an expensive club for a small group of doctors had been the day's activity.

Type of Event:	Example:
Real Events with an Improper Purpose	Events are planned and really take place, but with a different purpose than indicated. For example, if officials from the Administration of Industry and Commerce were giving the company a difficult time, the sales team might invite them on a tour of a company facility in Southern China and then use cash obtained through one of the other techniques described to send the attendees to a tourist destination like Macau.

Reports on the GSK case in Chinese and Western media allege that from 2007 to 2013, GSK personnel used a range of these approaches working with 700 different travel agencies to convey value totalling as much as ¥3 billion (about $476,190,000 at current exchange rates). Clearly, the travel agency model has (or had) scale!

Note, this tool has appeared in other China-related compliance cases, such as the IBM case brought by the US Securities & Exchange Commission in 2011. Whether the enforcement action against GSK will result in a significant change in the opportunity for travel agencies to serve as conduits for improper benefits remains to be seen. In the meanwhile, the administration of compliance programs for China operations should involve careful scrutiny of how travel agencies are being selected and used.

"White Glove"

If the GSK case has offered insights into ways commercial transactions can create enforcement risk, the year 2013 has also illustrated the ways officials in China manage their receipt of bribes. Two cases are emblematic of the manner in which Chinese officials are able to receive the benefit of bribes while (at least for a time) keeping their hands "clean." A term that developed in Taiwan has now spread to Mainland China to describe this approach: "white glove."

The white glove (白手套) is a private party who enjoys a close relationship with the official (or even more ideally, the official's family). The white glove either directly gives benefits to the official and his family, or acts for the official in bankrolling the schemes the official directs, all while covering and protecting the official so that the official's hands avoid getting sullied. Two cases prosecuted this year illustrate how this works.

As a giver of bribes to the official/family: In the prosecution of the disgraced Chongqing Party Secretary Bo Xilai, evidence was provided by Xu Ming, an entrepreneur from Dalian (where Bo was Party Secretary and Mayor in the early 1990's) that he had purchased a $3.2 million villa in the South of France for the Bo/Gu family, had paid expenses for Bo's son, Bo Guagua, to go on an expensive safari in Africa with friends and had paid Guagua's credit card charges when he studied overseas. Bo cross-examined Xu and multiple times Xu admitted that he never directly discussed these gifts with Bo. That may indeed have been true and if so, it would be consistent with the fiction that officials aim to create, that benefits are flowing to their family or friends, but that they do not extort or request these benefits.

As the intermediary for the official: Liu Zhijun is the former Railways Minister who has now been prosecuted and issued a suspended death sentence for his receipt of ¥64.6 million in bribes, a relatively small sum. However, his 'white glove', businesswoman Ding Shumiao, is believed to have held upwards of ¥2 billion for him. The prosecutors weren't able to show direct financial dealings between Ding and Liu, but that's not how the system works. Ding's companies acted as supplier/vendor for various inputs in constructing China's high-speed rail system. Liu helped ensure contracts were awarded to her and she used the high commissions she charged to amass a pool of funds that would be available to aid Liu in various ways.

One way Liu used the money was to direct Ding to bribe officials who were charged with investigating one of Liu's close associates for bribes. Another intended use of the funds, but one that was omitted from the final indictment, was that Liu was planning for Ding to bribe officials to secure his appointment to an even higher position in the government. Given that his position as Minister of Railways was already very senior, there are not that many people above Liu who would be in a position to decide an even higher appointment. In Ding's trial, it was reported that she gave more than ¥40 million in bribes to Fan Zengyu, the former director of the external investment office for poverty alleviation office under China's State Council (the State Council is analogous to the Cabinet in the US system). Ding stated that the funds were given to promote her as a philanthropist. An earlier version of the indictment stated that in Fan's role as director of the external investment office, he had access to international bank accounts and was the conduit for payments to a senior official. News reports have not speculated for whom Fan Zengyu, himself, may have been the 'white glove'. ...

And so the chain continues. Throughout, the official's hands stay clean until the Party decides to pursue him. Often, the investigators focus their efforts on pursuing the suspected 'white glove,' getting that person to provide evidence against the true target of the enforcement action. A Sichuan businessman who may be the 'white glove' for a former head of the Public Security Bureau (and erstwhile ally of Bo Xilai), Zhou Yongkan, was recently detained. What will 2014 bring?

The lessons from the Bo and Liu cases are many, but two are particularly important for foreign investors:

1. The good news respecting enforcement of 'official bribery' in China is that it tends to focus on the recipients of the bribes and their direct associates, so a foreign-invested company implicated in paying bribes, directly or indirectly, to an official is less likely to be prosecuted by PRC officials. Nevertheless, the strong media attention on these cases means they may come to the attention of foreign authorities, who may take an interest in investigating the givers of the bribes.
2. Be cautious of dealing with individuals who are highly-connected, (or who claim to be). Careful consideration should be given to the source and legitimacy of the individual's connections, as well as the ways they could go sour and impact your business.

Prepaid Gift Cards

The use of prepaid gift cards is exceedingly popular: sales of these cards in 2011 were estimated at more than ¥600 billion (around $90 million), with the market growing at an annual rate of 15% or higher. While prepaid gift cards have plenty of legitimate uses, they've also proven useful in tax avoidance, corruption and money laundering schemes. In 2012, 12 officials were prosecuted for embezzling government funds or receiving gift cards to secure memberships in high-end fitness clubs or cosmetic services at salons. For example, Yang Ping, former director of a business in the Beijing Municipal Finance Bureau, was prosecuted for accepting ¥558,000 ($89,442) in gift cards for fitness clubs and beauty parlors over a seven-year period. In 2011, the State Council issued a Notice indicating that governmental officials are prohibited from receiving commercial gift cards,[1] so to the extent your China team is suggesting that prepaid gift cards may make a suitable holiday courtesy gift to officials, you should recommend otherwise.

Underground Banks - Cashing Checks for Kickbacks

Underground banks don't just evade tax or currency restrictions. They also provide 'value added' services, like cashing checks to aid in paying kickbacks. As part of what was reported as the largest underground banking case in Beijing, one service provided by the 'banks' was to facilitate payment of kickbacks to tour guides. Chinese accounting rules are quite strict, thus when a well-known pharmacy chain sought to pay kickbacks to tour guides bringing guests in to purchase health supplements and medicines, it needed to think of how to do this. To make the payments in a manner allowing for them to be deducted by the pharmacy chain as a legitimate business expense, it issued checks to the tour guide who brought in the customer under the ubiquitous catch-all rubric, 'consulting services.' The tour guide would in turn go to the underground bank to cash the check and the bank would

---

[1] See *Anticorruption Transparency and Data Privacy: Competing Concerns in China's Regulation of Prepaid Gift Cards,* by Amy L. Sommers, Cecillia Dai and Michael A. Cumming, in K&L Gates Global Government Solutions 2013: Annual Outlook *available at* http://www.klgates.com/FCWSite/flash/ggs_report_2013_embed.htm#1, last visited October 4, 2013.

deduct a commission, no questions asked. Commissions for the underground banking services in cashing checks ranged from 0.3 - 0.8%: quite reasonable. One pharmacy chain calculated that over an 18 month period, it had issued checks totalling more than ¥36,000,000 (more than $5,700,000) to travel agents as kickbacks. Again, travel is a tricky area for compliance in China.

Conclusion

To borrow a phrase from the anxious professor character Mad-Eye Moody in the Harry Potter stories, the watchword in China should be 'vigilance - constant vigilance': almost endless creativity is brought to bear in devising ways to pay and receive bribes. Companies need to bring a similar level of creativity to the challenge of how to monitor and thwart efforts to do so in their name.

Amy L. Sommers is a U.S.-trained lawyer in Shanghai, and a partner at the law firm of K&L Gates. Her 25 year involvement in China began with the study of Mandarin and has developed into a deep appreciation of China's history, politics, culture and legal system. In the compliance field, Ms. Sommers' is a sought-after speaker, writer and advisor on the challenging issues associated with synthesizing legal requirements and business imperatives in China's fast-moving market.

Chapter Seven

Paying and Concealing Bribes to Customs Officials in Nigeria

Musikilu Mojeed

Multinational companies operating in Nigeria have long faced the difficult task of trying to move goods in and out of the country while withstanding bribery demands from corrupt customs officials. In this chapter, we explore situations where companies have unfortunately yielded to these demands and also offer advice for how your company can tow the narrow line of conducting business in Nigeria without behaving corruptly.

In 2002, three years after Nigeria returned to representative democracy after several years of military dictatorship, the Nigerian government constituted a panel to investigate and resolve violations of Nigerian law related to Temporary Import Permits (TIPs). TIPs are authorization documents that oil and gas services companies are required to obtain from the Nigeria Customs Service in order to import offshore drilling equipment, including rigs, into Nigeria on a temporary basis.

Once the Nigerian presidency announced the panel, Parker Drilling Company, a Delaware corporation that provides worldwide drilling services, rental tools and project management, knew that it was in big trouble.

In the months before the constitution of the panel, Parker Drilling had repeatedly violated Nigerian laws by bribing officials and then submitting false paperwork to the Nigerian Customs Service, a federal agency that assesses and collects duties and tariffs on goods and services imported into Nigeria. Under Nigerian law, oil rigs imported under a TIP are allowed to remain in Nigeria's waters for one year with a maximum of two six-month extensions.

In 2004, Parker exited Nigeria in ignominy after the resolution of the TIP Panel allowed the government to nationalize and ultimately sell the company's Nigerian rigs. On April 16, 2013, the company also entered into settlement with the Securities and Exchange Commission ("SEC"), agreeing to pay a disgorgement of $3,050,000 and a prejudgment interest of $1,040,818. It also consented to a final judgment permanently enjoining it from future Foreign Corrupt Practices Act ("FCPA") violations.

Parker Drilling is not the only company to have fallen prey to the bribery antics of customs officials in Nigeria and to have ended up paying huge fines to US regulators. From Parker Drilling to Panalpina, Tidewater to GlobalSantaFe, and Noble Corporation to Transocean, a large number of multinationals have paid dearly for succumbing to bribe demands by Nigerian Customs officials in exchange for false Temporary Import Permits.

It is little wonder though that foreign companies doing businesses in Nigeria are so likely to fall prey to demands for bribes by officials of the Nigeria Customs Service. The Customs Service is reputed for monumental and widespread corruption within its rank. Nigeria, a resource-rich country of about 170 million people, loses several billion naira annually as officials deliberately underestimate customs duties and import permits in exchange for hefty bribes. Hawking false TIP paperwork to companies operating in the oil and gas industry is growing more rampant. The question that presents itself therefore is this: how are bribes typically paid in Nigeria's customs world and how can companies avoid paying them?

Paper Moves and the Lure of Bribery

The most common method of bribery in Nigeria's customs service involves purchasing false paperwork. Noble Corporation, a Swiss company which provides offshore drilling services and equipment throughout the world, and trades on the New York Stock Exchange, agreed to a settlement with the SEC about three years ago after it was found to have paid bribes to obtain eleven false documentations from the customs officials to show export and re-import of its drilling rigs to and from Nigerian waters.

Noble's story is similar to Parker Drilling's in a lot of ways. Noble Drilling (Nigeria) Limited, a wholly owned subsidiary of Noble Corporation, was incorporated in Nigeria in September 1990 as an oil industry service company. Between January 2003 and May 2007, Noble-Nigeria had seven drilling rigs offshore of Nigeria. But rather than legitimately obtaining TIPs for the temporary import of its rigs into Nigerian waters, the company "relied on the paper process and authorized its customs agent to provide false documents to the Nigerian Customs Service," according to SEC filings. A "special handling charge" of at least $79,026 was made to the customs agent, who in turn passed a substantial portion of it to government officials in exchange for obtaining fake TIPs. The rigs didn't move as claimed in the false documentation and Noble, the SEC determined, made gains totaling at least $4,294,933 by operating rigs in Nigeria for the period it would have had to remove and re-import its rigs into the country as required by Nigerian law.

"Customs Overtime" and "Special Interventions"

The second element of the bribe is the concealment, the part that involves disguising the bribe on the company's own books and records. Between January 2002 and July 2007, GlobalSantaFe Corporation ("GSF"), an oil servicing company incorporated in the Cayman Islands but with headquarters in Texas, repeatedly bribed Nigerian customs officials, through its customs agents, to obtain false documentation for fake removal and re-importation of its oil rigs into Nigeria. The company also made a so-called "interventions" payment to customs officials in exchange for preferential treatment during the customs process. In at least four occasions, GSF engaged in "paper moves" purporting to have moved its rigs out of Nigeria after its TIPs expired, and then reimported them as required by Nigerian laws.

The company's books and records, however, told a different story. A $45,000 payment in October 2004, for example, was identified on its customer broker's invoice as an "intervention on consumables" for GSF's Adriatic VI rig. A $87,500 payment in late September 2004 to obtain a new TIP included a $3,500 bribe which was identified on the customs broker's invoice simply as "additional charges for export."

GSF was also found to have made other payments totaling approximately $300,000 to government officials in Gabon, Angola and Equatorial Guinea. The payments were concealed either as "official dues," "authorities fees," "customs escort," "customs pre-clearance," "interventions," "customs formalities," "customs fine," "customs overtime," or "customs vacation." In the end, GSF paid the price with the US authorities, agreeing to an injunction and payment of disgorgement amounting to $3,758,165 and a civil penalty of $2.1 million.

Other companies have also bowed to the Nigerian Customs officials' request for bribes by disguising illicit payments as legitimate expenses. Tidewater Incorporated, a publicly-traded company, used its Nigerian subsidiary, Tidex Nigeria Limited, to shell out approximately $1.6 million in bribes to officials to disregard certain regulatory requirements relating to the temporary importation of the company's vessels into Nigerian waters. The funds, disguised as "intervention payments" or "other vessel costs" on the company's books were passed to a Nigerian agent who, in turn, passed the funds to relevant officials. With bribes in their pockets, customs officials didn't care to apply sanctions when Tidewater's vessels arrived in Nigeria prior to the issuance of a TIP or were chartered to a new customer without cancelling and securing a new TIP.

Another company, Panalpina, a freight forwarding company headquartered in Switzerland that provides intercontinental air and ocean freight forwarding and logistics services, concealed payments in its books by labeling them as "local processing fees" and "special handling fees." The company also made "special" and "evacuation" payments in exchange for officials looking the other way regarding Nigerian customs regulations.

Paying Bribes to Avoid Import Duties

While the practice of engaging in paper moves and recycling rigs is rampant and well known, Transocean Incorporated, a corporation with headquarters in the Cayman Islands and Houston Texas, took its bribing antics a notch higher by also importing goods, including medicine, into Nigeria without paying duties. This is yet another form of bribery in Nigeria's customs world.

A SEC complaint indicates that between 2002 and 2007, Transocean passed bribes to customs officials, through Panalpina, and Panalpina's express door-to-door courier service, Pancourier. "From January 2002 to September 2005, Transocean used Pancourier 404 times to import various goods and materials into Nigeria without paying any customs duties to the Nigerian government," the document said. "The total invoiced amount for the 404 shipments was $472,341.87.

The complaint cited files maintained by Transocean as indicating that Pancourier invoiced Transocean for "local processing charges" after its parent company, Panalpina had "made arrangements" with Nigerian customs officials related to shipments on behalf of Transocean and others. Transocean was ultimately compelled to pay the SEC a disgorgement and prejudgment interest of $7,265,080 and the Department of Justice ("DOJ") a criminal fine of $13.44 million.

How to Avoid Paying Bribes in Nigeria

While most corporations are aware that corruption is widespread in Nigeria, it is nevertheless easy to be lured into the bribe-paying cycle. Nigerian partners, local staff contractors, consultants and even officials themselves, often try to impress on foreign companies that bribery is a customary way of doing business and that no one can do anything without greasing the palms of officials. Businesses might be told that making illicit payments helps them win contracts ahead of the competition, speed up customs processes, and reduce expenses on duties.

But corporations should also be aware that they need not yield to that kind of counsel. Ultimately, following the wrong path may put them in serious trouble with both Nigerian and other authorities. They would do better to take the precautions suggested below:

Due diligence on customs agents and other contractors hired in Nigeria

Bribery and other forms of corruption are rampant in Nigeria and corporations coming into the country for business need to determine whether local contractors they hire are those with sound business ethics. The best way to determine this is to commission due diligence on them with a view to determining whether they are free of any indictment, administrative sanction, regulatory action or engaged in unwholesome business practices. There are several Nigerian and non-Nigerian companies who offer due diligence services on Nigerian businesses and individuals. Reputable local experts are certainly worthwhile because they know the local market and its operators.

Anti-corruption training: Understanding Nigerian anti-corruption laws

One way to avoid falling prey to the bribery antics of Nigerian officials is for companies doing business in the country to periodically organize anti-corruption training for their local staff, local contractors and consultants. Personnel need to understand Nigerian anti-corruption laws and how to navigate Nigeria's Customs bureaucracy without paying bribes.

Local contractors who sometimes appear to profit the most from illicit payments to officials often create the impression that it is impossible to do business in Nigeria without paying bribes. This is not true, and employees should be made aware that Nigeria actually has stringent anti-corruption laws which could send violators to jail. It is important that staff familiarize themselves, for example, with the operations of the Economic and Financial Crimes Commission, the Independent Corrupt Practices and other Related Offences Commission, the Code of the Conduct Bureau, the Nigeria Police and other agencies.

It is important for them to know how to report demands for bribes to authorities. If trained and supported, employees can be a company's best defense system. Court papers say that in 2005, for example, after indications emerged that Panalpina was bribing customs officials to expedite customs clearance of its exports, Transocean requested its Nigeria-based employees to conduct an internal investigation of their use of Pancourier. In the course of the investigation, the employees met a Panalpina manager who admitted to Pancourier's unethical business practices. A report of the investigation was forwarded to Panalpina's executives in Houston who then put a policy in place allowing for only a limited use of Pancourier, and only with management pre-approval and proof of duty payments.

Be wary of corruption traps

Corporations should develop internal anti-corruption guidelines that will shield staff from falling prey to corruption traps. Any attempt to cut corners or unnecessarily speed things up, without following laid-down procedures, will almost certainly lead to corruption.

The best way to do business without compromising ethical obligations is by adhering to regulations and procedures. Some local customs agents and contractors may tell you that anything is possible as long as bribes are paid. They might also tell you that officials slow down things to compel corporations to pay bribes. Such offers and arguments are best rejected. Compliance teams must insist on the right and legal ways of doing things. For instance, corporations should not be desperate enough to move their rigs into Nigerian waters prior to the issuance of a Temporary Import Permit and they should not try to send vessels into Nigeria prior to obtaining a bond associated with a TIP.

Any company that tries to do paper moves of rigs or evade payments of legitimate custom charges will definitely fall for the bribe trap. For as long as companies insist on doing the right things in the right way, there will be no need to entice officials.

Understand legitimate customs charges

Corporations usually hire local customs agents, contractors and consultants to handle their customs-related transaction. This is often completely justifiable, but it is also important for key relevant officials, either on the ground in Nigeria, or far away in foreign headquarters, to familiarize themselves with legitimate local business and customs charges. This will help in raising red flags when illicit payments are invoiced for payment. The legitimate customs charges should be itemized, possibly tabulated and circulated to all staff that deal with customs and customs agents on behalf of the company. All other charges not reflected in the document should be rejected until they can be verified.

This was a red flag that Parker Drilling failed to address. According to the SEC complaint in the case, on April 13, 2004, a Nigerian agent emailed a Parker official saying, "There is nothing more serious... I have [a] meeting tomorrow in Abuja to discuss the drilling contracts. This is my reason for making sure that I can entertain my hosts because of their promises. Therefore, please make sure that you transfer the funds today so that my Bank Officer can send it to Nigeria tomorrow." Earlier, on February 24, 2004, the agent had sent an email, saying, "I need to spend another $60,000 on public relations for the intelligence work and this will be paid when the [home use] concession is given. We will need SSS (Nigeria's secret police – State Security Service) in the future. It will help me if the US$100,000 is sent to my account..." These kinds of urgent, eleventh hour requests for large sums of money are often a sign of suspicious behavior.

Close monitoring of local and expatriate staff

Corporations need also to pay attention to the conduct of their Nigeria-based staff. Some staffs collude with custom agents and contractors to carry out bribery schemes for their own gain. Do any staff members appear to be living obviously beyond their pay grade?

It is also important that expatriate staff not be allowed to remain in one post for too long. When that happens, they get used to the customary ways of doing things, and then can develop cover-up schemes. It helps that staff are rotated with financial and operational audit done each time a key expatriate departs.

Conclusion

Navigating the hugely corrupt Nigeria Customs Service presents a tough challenge for corporations attempting to remain compliant with the Foreign Corrupt Practices Act and other anti-corruption laws. But it is possible to avoid the bribery tricks of corrupt customs officials and their collaborators. Businesses and their personnel only need to learn how to counter bribe demands and operate without compromising themselves. Once a company is known for its anti-corruption stance, even the most chronic bribe solicitors will learn to do business with it using only legitimate methods.

Musikilu Mojeed is Managing Editor at Nigeria's multimedia newspaper, *Premium Times*. Until 2011, he was Investigative Editor at Nigeria's *NEXT* newspaper where he directed the groundbreaking investigative work of that newspaper and coordinated the paper's WikiLeaks coverage. Mr. Mojeed is also a recent J.S. Knight Journalism Fellow at Stanford University. Before then, he was a Ford Foundation International Fellow at The City University of New York. He has reported extensively on corruption, human rights and human trafficking in Africa.

Chapter Eight

Regional Flavor: Crosscutting Corruption Issues in Latin America

Matteson Ellis[1]

While corruption is illegal in every country of the world, the form it takes may vary from region to region. Regional considerations for bribery and corruption risks include the size of the economic market, the strength of state governments and the local business culture. In other chapters of the book, we looked at corruption patterns in China and Nigeria; now, we focus our attention on Latin America.

In many ways, bribery in Latin America looks like bribery anywhere else. An unscrupulous businessperson sees an opportunity to get ahead by giving kickbacks to government officials. A corrupt official extracts personal concessions while performing public sector duties. At the same time, corrupt acts often manifest themselves through specific local "flavors" – homegrown, personal ways of running corruption schemes.

But what are the common, crosscutting issues that lend a distinctive regional flavor to corruption in Latin America? In my experience working on corruption in the region, I have identified

[1] The author would like to thank Matthew Fowler and Carlos Ayres for their support with editing. The views expressed here are Mr. Ellis's personally and do not express the views of Miller & Chevalier Chartered.

five issues that I think significantly inform the way bribes are paid there: boom and bust economic cycles, the prevalence of state-owned companies, weak government institutions, concentrations of wealth and power in a small elite, and family ownership of companies. These areas are closely interrelated and tend to reinforce one another.

Whether you are in the concrete jungles of Mexico City or the Amazonian jungles of northwestern Brazil, these characteristics, and the types of corrupt behavior they encourage, seem to persist. As described below, understanding them is key to identifying and avoiding corruption risks in the region.

The Effects of Boom and Bust Economic Cycles

Boom and bust cycles are a common occurrence in Latin America. My first time to experience this was when I moved to Argentina in 1998. At that time, the country's economy was experiencing a high level of growth and foreign investment. General Motors, my employer, had recently chosen to build a new, state-of-the-art manufacturing plant there. This enthusiasm for Argentina centered around the country's newfound monetary stability. President Menem's economic team had pegged the Argentine peso to the U.S. dollar, a notable development considering the country's history of hyperinflation.

But over the span of a few years, the economic system unraveled before my eyes. The disciplined monetary policy limited the competitiveness of Argentina's exports and widespread corruption surrounding privatization of state-owned enterprises deprived the country of important public funds, and the government of credibility. The hard currency peg became unsustainable, and when the government let the exchange rate float freely, the peso lost more than half of its value almost overnight. Foreign capital fled, bank accounts were frozen, and the country spiraled into economic chaos. A wave of popular protests forced one president, Fernando de la Rúa, out of office. He was succeeded by three more presidents in the span of a few weeks. Latin America had experienced yet another boom and bust cycle.

Latin America is known for such periods of economic expansion followed by precipitous collapses. A boost in commodity prices in the 1970s led to economic growth that abruptly ended in a sharp debt crisis in the early 1980s. Market-oriented reforms in the early 1990s created a surge in short-term capital that ended in the Tequila crisis of 1994.

These cycles have devastating impacts on the region's people. They also color corruption risks for foreign companies doing business there. During a rising tide, competition goes up. Companies ask fewer questions about the practices of their employees. They demand quicker results to stay ahead. In addition, local officials see more opportunity for personal gain. When opportunity grows at such a rapid pace, there is little motivation for governments to root out wrongdoing. Adding to the challenge, regulations do not tend to keep up with innovation. As a result, improper business practices that might be tolerated locally assert themselves with greater frequency. Overall, corruption risk goes up.

The nature of corruption takes on a different character when booms turn to busts. The downslope can be especially steep in under-regulated economies. Politicians may make dramatic – or "revolutionary" – changes to regulatory bodies, rather than incremental changes to existing institutions. This undermines the quality of institutions, and public faith in them. It also tends to emphasize the importance of individuals and personal relationships over a commonly accepted system of rules in an economic sector.

When economies contract, the schemes that accompanied prior growth are often exposed as well. Politicians look for someone to blame, and foreign companies become easy targets. This can lead to nationalizations resulting in state-ownership of key sectors and industries of the economy, which creates another unique set of corruption risks, discussed later in this chapter.

As a result of these cycles, politicians are able to avoid accountability, both on the upswing and the downswing. They avoid scrutiny in boom times, and they avert blame during downturns. Booms and busts also reinforce inequalities among the region's people, since the poor and middle classes are affected most by the downturns. The resulting concentrations of money and power also affect corruption risk, as discussed later in this chapter.

These dynamics suggest that companies should be alert during the economic booms and busts that regularly play out in the region. Brazil, "the "B" in the world's BRIC countries, is a good example. Macroeconomic stability there has generated consistent GDP growth for several years. The country's GDP is now larger than that of the United Kingdom. The GDP is only about 10% smaller than that of France. But the seeds might be sown for a future bust, especially considering the country's complicated dynamics. On one hand, it is far from a "Banana Republic," to borrow the pejorative term sometimes used to describe underdeveloped Latin American economies that have traditionally been dependent on the U.S. economy. On the other, it is not quite a highly mature and developed economy like, say, that of Canada. Brazil is a unique mix. It now has a large and modern private sector and relatively weak government institutions. Returns on investment are impressive. So are poverty rates and infrastructure gaps.

These conditions should make foreign companies wary. Not only should they expect to find a sophisticated and savvy business sector in Brazil, but they also need to watch out for corruption schemes that might hide beneath the surface. Price fixing and collusion between competitors and elaborate manipulation of public bids using multiple parties are just some of the types of common schemes found in the country. Opportunities for corruption are heightened given the huge investment-laden global events like the World Cup and Olympics that will be held there in the coming years. While these events are evoking notions of exciting national competition, they are also prompting serious questions about investment decisions and how construction and redevelopment projects are being allocated. For example, concerns have been raised over the decision to build a $270 million World Cup soccer stadium in the middle of the Amazon, in a city surrounded by a rain forest that stretches for around 2.1 million square miles. When the events are over, will these investments be seen as long-term productive assets for Brazil? Or will they join a parade of "white elephant" projects in the region?

These types of booms are occurring not only in Brazil but throughout the region. Colombia's newfound security has led to a foreign investment rate of 28% of GDP, the highest level in a decade. With Peru's extensive deposits of gold, zinc, copper, and other valuable minerals, the country has experienced the second highest increase of foreign direct investment in percentage terms and the second highest GDP growth in the region. Such booms should be greeted with caution.

Prevalence of State Ownership

Foreign companies doing business in Latin America commonly encounter state ownership and control of businesses in sectors usually dominated by private companies in other parts of the world, including the United States. Similarly, state-owned companies in Latin America often act like private businesses – particularly if they have been recently nationalized. The trend is common. Argentina recently nationalized the country's main oil company, YPF. Venezuela's government recently went so far as to take control of a toilet paper company to address a nationwide shortage. This heightened role of the state gives rise to heightened bribery risks.

When governments tighten control over the economy, foreign companies are forced to confront more touch-points with government officials in their regular business, which increases bribery risk. Officials can exercise more leverage over private companies given the government's dominance in the market. This presents more opportunities for government officials to extract rents. Some normal business practices become higher risk. For example, standard marketing practices like giving gifts, meals, entertainment, and business travel can become unduly problematic. While these activities can be entirely legitimate in business for purposes of building relationships and goodwill, they can also be performed with corrupt intent.

The 2011 action by the U.S. Department of Justice and the U.S. Securities and Exchange Commission against reinsurance company Aon under the U.S. Foreign Corrupt Practices Act (FCPA) is a good example. It ended in a $16.2 million settlement for bribes paid by the company in Costa Rica, Panama, and other developing countries.

In general, reinsurers like Aon provide insurance for insurance companies, and they usually have a particular interest in working for state-owned insurance companies that have monopolies, like the ones of Central America. This is because such companies control considerable market share and are highly exposed when a catastrophic event like a volcano, earthquake, or hurricane occurs. To spread the risk, state companies purchase reinsurance policies. When this happens, reinsurance companies must teach their clients about the complicated products they sell so that clients can make sound decisions based on their own particular needs. When insurers better evaluate risk, everyone benefits.

But at some point, trainings offered to state-owned clients can turn into bribes under the FCPA if not accompanied by proper controls. For example, Aon's "Training and Education Fund" was originally created to educate employees of the Costa Rican state-owned insurance company. Over time, it started being used for boondoggles. Seminars in Monte Carlo had no connection to the business of insurance. Resulting expenses were not recorded accurately on Aon's books and records, creating additional liabilities.

The procurement practices of state-owned companies are also particularly problematic because they involve a transfer of public dollars to private entities. Large amounts of money are at stake when the government procures things like roads, computer systems, oil extraction services, medical equipment, power stations, and textbooks. The incentives to manipulate the process can be great.

Officials may, for example, do any of the following:
- steer valuable contracts to companies willing to pay kickbacks;
- require bidders to hire "consultants" as a way of funneling funds back to their own accounts;
- narrowly design a project's specifications as a way to ensure that the bribe-paying bidder wins; or
- disqualify other non-bribe-paying bidders on highly technical grounds to clear the field.

Bidders, on the other hand, may have their own corrupt practices, including:
- hiring officials for bogus consulting engagements as a way to transfer improper funds to them;
- hiring an "expert" who previously worked for the procurement agency who can serve as an easy conduit of bribe payments; or
- illicitly gaining access to a competitor's bid to fashion a winning bid.

These types of risks are evident in the number of FCPA enforcement actions that have involved public procurements in Latin America. Siemens is illustrative. In Venezuela, the company admitted to paying bribes through a series of consultants to obtain contracts to design and build mass rail transit systems worth hundreds of thousands of dollars. In Argentina, it admitted to paying tens of millions of dollars, some through consultants, to obtain a contract to provide national identity cards to the country, valued at around $1 billion.

Weak Government Institutions

Latin America is often characterized by weak government institutions. They can generate corruption risk in a variety of ways. For example, the lack of credible institutions can encourage impunity. It can also complicate the ability of governments to administer the wide variety of complex government regulations that apply to businesses throughout the region.

In particular, bribery thrives when there are not effective institutions to expose, investigate, judge, and penalize it. It is common in the region for judicial systems to lack professionalism and independence. The police are also often seen as the problem, not the solution. In the 2012 Latin America Corruption Survey conducted by fourteen law firms throughout the Americas, the police were found to create the highest consistent bribery risk of any government area in Latin America, no matter the country. Police risk was most pronounced in Mexico, Venezuela, and Peru.

These factors lead to high degrees of impunity throughout the region. Nearly three-quarters of respondents to the 2012 Latin America Corruption Survey stated that anti-corruption laws were ineffective in the countries where they worked. When people see little risks associated with engaging in corrupt activity, the activity can flourish.

Indeed, in many countries, the same government institutions charged with fighting corruption are the very ones implicated in corruption. For example, in 2013, U.S. authorities arrested Bolivia's top anti-corruption police official in Miami for attempting to extort bribes from a Bolivian businessperson cooperating with the FBI. *The Miami Herald's* news commentator Andres Oppenheimer pointed out in a column that the most telling thing about the event was not necessarily the official's act, or his arrest, but instead the fact that the event was not covered in any depth by major newspapers, including *The Miami Herald*, *The New York Times*, or *El Nuevo Herald*. Was the event really this commonplace?

The negative effects of weak institutions are also dramatic given the high levels of poor regulatory quality directly affecting businesses in the region. Latin America is known for its Byzantine and costly regulatory regimes. The World Bank's Doing Business 2012 report ranks Latin American countries, on average, in the bottom half worldwide for regulatory quality. The report compares 183 economies by measuring the clarity, predictability, and efficiency of regulations that apply to areas like construction permits, getting electricity, registering property, getting credit, protecting investors, and paying taxes.

Complex regulations demand capable institutions. In their absence, opportunities grow for public officials to demand bribes. When such rules are not clear, public officials have more discretion in their decision-making. Ambiguity creates opportunities to manipulate rules for corrupt purposes. The more government actors are involved in the process, the greater the chances a company will face bribe requests. Complex regulatory regimes also mean that companies must often rely on *despachantes* (middlemen), *gestores* (facilitators), or other third party agents to get things done. Without proper vetting and controls, these third parties can make improper payments on a company's behalf.

It is common for essential private institutions to be weak too. In general, the free press should play a key role in ensuring accountability of government, which works to mitigate corruption risk. It can expose wrongdoing and create an important deterrent effect. But in Latin America, the press is not always allowed to play its proper role. Between 2008 and 2013, the non-governmental organization Freedom House reported consecutive declines in press freedom in the region. State-led repression of private media outlets and violence against journalists were found to affect over 60 percent of the region's Spanish-speaking countries.

Concentrations of Wealth and Power

Latin America is known as one of the most economically unequal regions of the world. By 2010, according to United Nations Development Program data, Latin America had 18 of the 25 countries in the world with the most disparate income distributions. And throughout Latin America, it is common to find government and business dominated by a relatively small number of elite families. Their members move in and out of government and business, creating complex financial and political relationships. This elevates corruption risks in several ways.

First, it increases the risk of collusion within a particular sector or industry. There is a good chance that the leaders of the primary market participants will be connected to each other in some way. This can facilitate arrangements such as price-fixing and manipulation of public procurements accomplished through clustered bid quotes, coordinated unit cost schedules, and rotating contract awards.

Second, it increases the likelihood that foreign companies will wind up interacting with government officials in ways they might not expect. For example, I worked with an international company using a local law firm in Central America only to discover that one of its partners concurrently served in the government in a way that raised bribery concerns. Another U.S. company planned to partner with a Mexican firm only to discover that the owner's brother served a key position in government vis a vis the same industry. Where a local company's business stops and the government starts might not always be clearly demarcated.

Another risk associated with high concentrations of wealth and power relates to monopolies. When power is in the hands of a few, it is common for one single company to dominate an entire industry in a small country. In larger countries, one company might dominate a regional segment of a national market. Questions might be raised about how the company got in the position of dominance in the first place. Risks also arise when a foreign investor is forced to rely on the monopoly for its business. To manage such risks, companies are expected to conduct anti-corruption due diligence on their partners. Obtaining compliance certifications, audit rights, and the like is difficult when the partner is the only option in the market. Foreign companies will often lack the leverage to demand compliance assurances.

Finally, divisions in wealth have the effect of facilitating petty corruption. When low-level government officials are not paid enough, they sometimes rationalize seeking rent by other means. Bribe requests might be baked into the economic order. The 2012 Americas Barometer Study, conducted by the Latin American Public Opinion Project, polled over 40,000 people in 26 countries throughout the region. Each country involved a minimum of 1,500 polling interviews. Many of the questions were designed to measure corruption victimization by low-level officials, like police officers, municipal permitting officials, and hospitals and clinics. These are the types of everyday bribe requests that affect the average citizen. Overall, a startling 57% of respondents throughout the entire region said they had experienced at least one instance of low-level corruption in the prior year. Forty-three percent (43%) were repeat victims.

Family Ownership of Companies

Family ownership of companies is common in Latin America. One study from the University of São Paulo concluded that half of Brazil's 200 largest companies are owned by families. This can be explained in part by structural factors, like the relative weakness of local laws designed to protect minority shareholder rights, which makes it difficult for family companies to attract outside investors. The relative prominence of family-owned companies can have direct effects on corruption risk.

For example, foreign companies making investments in the region will often find themselves partnering with companies that lack common accounting standards, corporate governance transparency, or basic internal controls. This can complicate the ability of outsiders to perform the type of anti-corruption due diligence necessary to manage corruption risks in mergers and acquisitions. Moreover, a family might feel offended at the prospect of having to be vetted for corruption issues, even if it has nothing to hide. It might be reluctant to open up its books and operations to outside lawyers and accountants. As a result, those negotiating the deal might need to factor in time to explain why anti-corruption due diligence is necessary as an evolving business requirement of international work.

Working through these issues requires sustained attention and cultural understanding. For example, integrating a local family-owned company into an acquiring company's anti-corruption compliance program usually demands care. In one case, a colleague working in compliance needed to be embedded in the local family-owned company for six months after an acquisition, specifically to oversee compliance integration. She said that she could not have done her job successfully without a high degree of cultural sensitivity. This meant listening to local employees more often than dictating to them, knowing when and when not to introduce new compliance concepts and correct lingering misunderstandings, sensing when to concede issues and when to push back, and artfully generating buy-in from the company's various sectors. It meant first building respect and trust through personal relationships. She made it a priority to attend dinners and family gatherings with her local colleagues. She slowly educated the company on the stakes associated with non-compliance and the rationale behind anti-bribery rules. At the end of the day, the compliance integration proved successful.

Conclusion

Corruption is a crime of opportunity. People pay bribes by exploiting weaknesses. The five areas listed in this chapter – boom and bust economic cycles, the prevalence of state-owned companies, weak government institutions, concentrations of wealth and power in a small elite, and family ownership of companies – all create common opportunities for corruption to occur in Latin America. Understanding these dynamics helps give non-Latin American businesspeople an understanding of, and appreciation for, some of the unique flavors of the region.

Matteson Ellis is Special Counsel to Miller & Chevalier Chartered in Washington, DC with extensive experience in anti-corruption compliance and enforcement, including the U.S. Foreign Corrupt Practices Act (FCPA). He has worked on anti-corruption matters in multiple capacities, including prevention, detection, remediation, investigation, defense, and enforcement. Mr. Ellis has performed complex, independent, and on-site internal investigations in over 20 countries throughout the Americas, Asia, Europe, and Africa considered "high corruption risk" by international monitoring organizations. He has investigated fraud and corruption and supported administrative sanctions and debarment proceedings for The World Bank and The Inter-American Development Bank. He focuses particularly on the Americas, is fluent in Spanish and Portuguese, regularly speaks on corruption matters throughout the region, and is Founder and Editor of the FCPAméricas Blog (www.fcpamericas.com).

Chapter Nine

From Favors to Bribes: The Social Context of Corruption in Nigeria

Daniel Jordan Smith

While most Nigerians condemn large-scale corruption and the global internet scams for which Nigeria is notorious, in this chapter Daniel Jordan Smith, a professor of anthropology at Brown University, describes the everyday forms of corruption that are prevalent in Nigerian society. These "accepted" forms of corruption, including bribes euphemistically called "dashes," contribute to a social universe in which much more egregious forms of corruption are justified and, thereby, tolerated.

To explain the prevalence and durability of bribery in Nigeria, it is necessary to understand the ways that average Nigerians who condemn corruption also participate in its perpetuation. Through examining the everyday workings of corruption in their most mundane forms it becomes possible to see how Nigerians can be both critics of and complicit participants in corrupt schemes, even as they are also victims. The involvement of ordinary Nigerians in petty corruption makes it more difficult to mobilize the collective political action necessary to combat large-scale corruption that is obviously so detrimental to Nigeria and its people.

"Settling" Oga

When Nigerians seek a service from their government they routinely expect that they will have to navigate corruption at all levels of the bureaucracy. Everything from obtaining birth and death certificates, to registering a company, to applying for a passport, to renewing a motor vehicle registration typically requires some sort of illicit payment in addition to the official fee. Generally, the only way to avoid paying extra money for routine government services is to use a personal connection to someone with influence – a patron who will use his power to push on behalf of his client. But even then, a relationship of reciprocity exists: the patron is helping with the implicit expectation that his act contributes to retaining and strengthening the loyalty of his client. Further, although a friendly patron who helps a client navigate the bureaucracy may not expect payment, the client will nonetheless frequently offer a "dash" (a more socially acceptable term for a bribe) to say "thank you." Indeed, part of the complexity of official corruption in Nigeria is the way that the mechanisms of bureaucracy become personalized, even in situations where citizen and bureaucrat are, in fact, complete strangers.

My experience registering a car in Nigeria is illustrative. I bought the car in Owerri, the capital of Imo State in southeastern Nigeria. Frank, my friend and research assistant, had spent a whole day with me looking at used cars and he helped me decide which one to buy. Frank agreed to accompany me the next morning to the licensing office to register the vehicle and apply for a driver's license. I told Frank that I wanted to get the registration and driver's license as quickly as possible. My past experience suggested that Nigerian bureaucrats tend to have one of two reactions to requests for services from foreigners. Either they are embarrassed or afraid to request bribes from an expatriate and therefore render the service more easily than to fellow Nigerians, or they see a foreigner as an opportunity to inflate the Nigerian prices and get even more money, over and above both the official and unofficial fees. As Frank and I parked at the licensing office in Owerri, I hoped for the former, but expected the latter.

The office for registration of vehicles consisted of two rooms at the back of a large office block. In the first room were four desks, each piled with files. Behind each desk sat Nigerian civil servants. As we entered the room a woman at the back desk was typing something on an old manual typewriter, and a man at the front desk was entering figures in a ledger. Two other people had their heads on their arms on top of their desks as if they were napping. After greeting everyone, I asked who we should see about registering a car. The man entering figures in his ledger perked up. "C.A. Okonkwo," he said, standing and holding out his hand to shake mine, "I am in charge of vehicle registration." I explained to Mr. Okonkwo that I had just purchased a car and I wanted to register it and apply for a driver's license. "Of course," he said. Then Mr. Okonkwo's face grew somber. "Unfortunately," he continued, "there are no number plates. Imo State plates are finished." Frank immediately jumped in, knowing from experience that scarcity, whether real or faked, was a typical ploy for a bureaucrat to seek a bribe. "Mr. Dan is our in-law," Frank announced. "He is just as much a Nigerian as you or me. You should treat him as a brother. We need the registration and plates as soon as possible." With these few words Frank had communicated to Mr. Okonkwo both that I knew that I might have to "put something on top" (as officials often euphemistically say when requested a bribe) of the official fees to get efficient service, and that he should not try to take undue advantage of my being a foreigner. We were willing to pay a dash, but we would not be swindled.

When Frank announced that I was an in-law, the women who appeared to be napping on their desks sat up and we all engaged in a friendly discussion that included a brief story of how I met my wife. I reinforced my desired "almost Nigerian" status by switching my speech to the Igbo language. I gladly engaged in these minutes of friendly banter because I had long ago learned that the more personal I could make my relationships with Nigerian bureaucrats, the more likely they would be to treat me like a fellow Nigerian. I would still have to "put something on top," but I would be less likely to be cheated by Nigerian standards.

Once everyone was satisfied that I really was an in-law, Mr. Okonkwo returned to the business at hand. "Imo State plates are finished," he said, "but I can get plates from Anambra State if you require urgent service." I told him I wanted urgent service so long as the price was fair. I informed him that I also needed the driver's license just as quickly. "Ah," Mr. Okonkwo sighed, "that might be a problem because the machine that produces the licenses is temporarily out of service." Frank and I exchanged smiles. "How much would it cost to put the machine back in service," Frank asked. "Well, for five thousand naira our in-law can have his driver's license tomorrow," Mr. Okonkwo replied, as if his offer were generous. Frank then said to Mr. Okonkwo, "See, oga (oga is a common Nigerian word for "boss" or "big man"), just tell us the price for everything – the driver's license, the number plates, the insurance, and all the clearances so that Mr. Dan will not be hassled by the police. If we agree on the price, then you will do everything. You will be the one who settles all those people. We just want to collect everything tomorrow." Frank's reference to the clearances was a key part of the transaction. In addition to the actual vehicle registration certificate, Nigerian drivers are expected to carry several other official documents, including one that verifies that the police have determined the vehicle is not stolen. Without all the proper documents one is likely to be delayed at police checkpoints with demands for money in lieu of the proper papers. Each of these documents has its own bureaucracy and officials who need to be "settled" – the Nigerian English verb for paying an expected dash, bribe, or kickback.

After doing some rough calculations, Mr. Okonkwo handed me a piece of paper with a large amount written down. Frank and I both shouted "heh!" to express our assessment that the amount was too high. Over a period of a few minutes, Frank called me aside to discuss how much I would be willing to pay and then called Mr. Okonkwo aside to discuss how much he would be willing to take. Eventually, we agreed on a price. Mr. Okonkwo wanted all the money up front. I was reluctant because this left me with little leverage and no recourse if he failed to deliver as promised, but Frank convinced me I should go ahead. At least Mr. Okonkwo did not ask me to leave my car with him, I thought, naively imagining that the police might actually want to see the car to check whether or not it had been stolen. Mr. Okonkwo promised to have everything by the following afternoon.

When Frank and I showed up the next day, Mr. Okonkwo did not have the plates. He said that he had traveled to Anambra State only to find that their plates were also out of stock. But not to worry, he said, the Anambra officials assured him that in Ebonyi State plates were available, and if I gave him some additional money for transportation he would procure my plates by tomorrow. Frank suspected that he was simply trying to exploit me and angrily told Mr. Okonkwo that we had a deal and that it was his responsibility to get the plates, whatever that meant. Mr. Okonkwo grumbled but seemed to accept the notion of a binding bargain, even based on a bribe, and he told us to come back the next day. Sure enough, the following day I had Ebonyi State plates and all the proper documents for my car. The only thing Mr. Okonkwo hadn't given me was my driver's license, for which five thousand naira had been included in the deal. "What about my driver's license," I asked. Again Mr. Okonkwo frowned. "The machine is still not working," he said. "You can drive with your temporary receipt until the machine is fixed." I knew a temporary receipt would work because in the 1990s I had driven in Nigeria for nearly two years using just such a temporary license, and I was ready to resign myself to waiting again for the real one. But Frank was irate. He suspected that Mr. Okonkwo had simply pocketed the extra money for the urgent processing of the driver's license rather than "settling" whoever operated the machine. He demanded that Mr. Okonkwo accompany us to the office where drivers' licenses were issued.

Reluctantly, Mr. Okonkwo followed us to another office. After the usual greetings I explained to the woman in charge that I had applied for a driver's license and that Mr. Okonkwo had promised it for the previous day. I pleaded with her to issue my license. She asked her secretary to bring my file and then explained that the computer and printer that produce the plastic licenses required electricity and the office had received no electricity for several days. Once there was electricity, she said, I would have my license. "What about the generator?" I asked. I had seen a small gasoline-powered electricity generator outside her office, obviously available precisely because the national power supply was so fickle. "No petrol," she said. At that moment Frank asked me to excuse them. Moments later Frank emerged and said that I could come the next day to collect my license. When I asked what he had said to them in my absence Frank reported that he told the woman that we had already paid enough money "on top" to get the license urgently and that it was up to Mr. Okonkwo to settle her and assure that my license was issued immediately. She was apparently irritated with Okonkwo for "eating alone" (not sharing the unofficial dash we had paid for efficient service), and promised Frank that the license would be ready the next day. I have no idea how much Mr. Okonkwo had to pay to assuage the licensing officer.

The next day I came back to the office optimistic that I would finally get my driver's license. When I asked for Mr. Okonkwo, his colleagues said that he was "not on seat," but that the overall boss wanted to see me – a woman I had not yet met. I entered her office with a big smile and a warm greeting, hoping my friendliness would spare me from having to settle anyone else. Holding my plastic driver's license in her hand, she asked, "So Mr. Smith, you wanted to collect all your papers and your license without ever seeing me?" I tried to feign ignorance, pretending not to know that by "seeing" her she meant "settling" her – "seeing" being a well-known synonym for "settling." I told her that I was happy to see her and that I had intended no offence. After all, I said, I would never want to avoid my in-laws, attempting to change the register of our conversation from that between a bureaucrat and service seeker to one between two in-laws. Fortunately for me, it seemed to work and as she handed me my license she said, "In future, you should see me, not just my staff." "Of course, madam," I said, as I departed happy to finally have my license. As difficult as it was to get my vehicle documentation, without the extra money I paid, and without the aid of Frank, I might have waited weeks for these services, wasting valuable time with regular trips to the licensing office, only to be frustrated.

The help I received from Frank was out of friendship, but many Nigerians find navigating government bureaucracies frustrating and people frequently rely on the aid of middlemen. Indeed, at almost every major bureaucracy that provides essential services, one finds a small army of middlemen ready to expedite one's business. Nigerians sometimes derisively call these middlemen "touts," the same derisive name used to describe the urban urchins who populate lorry parks and bus stations trying to make a few cents shepherding people onto public transportation. Touts can be either employees of the bureaucracy or private entrepreneurs who have developed connections in the office that enable them to navigate the bureaucracy effectively. A good middleman can save a service seeker time and money. But some middlemen don't deliver what they promise, especially if their connections are not what they advertise, or if they try to skirt settling their own patrons. Mr. Okonkwo's failure to settle the woman who issued the driver's license, or to share any of my money with his own boss, exemplifies this kind of problem. While middlemen offer valuable services in the face of a corrupt bureaucracy, they are sometimes excessively venal and unscrupulous in their dealings with the public and add yet another layer of interests invested in preserving practices of corruption.

It is necessary to point out that the story of my encounter with bureaucratic corruption is incomplete. I tell it purely from the perspective of a citizen (or in this case an alien) seeking government services. It is just as important to understand the perspective of the civil servants who sit behind those desks and expect to receive "something on top." Typically, Nigerian civil servants are poorly paid, and salaries are often not remitted on time. At the time I applied for my license, civil servants in Imo State had not been paid for four months. People like Mr. Okonkwo sometimes rely on the money they make through corruption to feed their families. Furthermore, civil servants frequently have to provide services to people to whom they have affective or social obligations, such as kin or friends, without receiving anything "on top." They might even be expected to provide services without collecting the official fees, since people in their networks may expect this help as a perceived benefit of having someone well placed in the bureaucracy. To refuse to help would risk being branded a bad person in a social world where an ethics of reciprocal exchange is highly valued. Thus, while civil servants collecting bribes to do their jobs are certainly using a public office for personal gain, they are often doing so in contexts of strong economic and social pressures. Central to any long-term solution to corrupt bureaucracies is not only greater transparency and accountability, but also fair pay for the employees who use low or late wages as an excuse to set their own fees on the side.

Extortion by (the Police) Force

My concern with obtaining all the correct paperwork for my car reflected 15 years of driving experience in Nigeria, and the awareness that the police are regularly looking for justifications to extort money from motorists. As a foreigner, I was less likely to experience outright threats of violence from the police than if I were Nigerian, but more likely to have my papers examined for any a hint of impropriety, looking for some justification to extract cash. In Nigeria, as in many societies, perhaps the most notorious and popularly despised examples of everyday corruption are police roadside checkpoints.

Nigerian police and soldiers routinely set up roadblocks at which vehicles are stopped, drivers besieged, and passengers hassled. Nigerians are subjected to police and military checkpoints daily, and anyone who travels on Nigeria's roads, whether in private cars or public transportation, will encounter them frequently. Most people interpret these checkpoints as means for police and soldiers to extract money from the public, symbolizing larger processes of control through which the powerful enrich themselves at the expense of the wider population.

Interactions with the police at roadside checkpoints usually unfold according to a common script, with which nearly all Nigerians are familiar. After being stopped by a barricade or a pointed weapon, police demands for money take several forms, including some in the euphemism of a polite request. Typical ways Nigerian police ask for money include: "Any weekend for us?" "We are loyal sir," "Give us something for cigarettes," "Any 'pure water'?" "Any 'roger' today?" or simply "I salute you," followed by a look of expectation. When the Nigerian police or military say "roger me," alluding to how the word "roger" is used in radio communication – as in "roger, over and out" – all Nigerians know that in order for the encounter to end, the officer requires payment. The reference to "pure water," like the reference to cigarettes, is meant to imply that the request is small – "pure water" being the name for sachets of drinking water sold all over Nigeria for a few pennies.

The often friendly nature of the request for "something small" is belied by the guns and by the behavior of the police when one fails to comply, or when they are simply in a bad mood. In such cases, instead of a polite request, the driver of a private vehicle is, for example, likely to hear, "clear well" or "park well" followed by a demand to see "your particulars" (meaning vehicle documents and license). Official documents are examined to look for any omission or mistake, and if one is found the cost of continuing one's journey is inflated. Even when all is in order, a "hungry" policeman might demand to look under the hood, supposedly checking the engine and chassis numbers against what is written on the vehicle registration. The longer the delay, the more likely drivers will offer something just for the chance to get going.

For commercial vehicles, the routine is streamlined. It is expected that the driver or his conductor will pay a small amount at every checkpoint, and usually this happens without delay or incident. Bus and taxi loads of passengers collectively condemn the police at virtually every checkpoint. But a driver who fails to pay will also be condemned for delaying his passengers. Despite the routine nature of these payments, several times a year the

Nigerian press reports incidents where the police shoot and kill a driver or conductor over disputes escalating from transactions at checkpoints. The fact that corruption at police checkpoints occasionally ends in violence reinforces why ordinary citizens resent this form of corruption so deeply, even though the amounts of money are small. Money paid at police checkpoints amount to a kind of toll or levy, in which no service is rendered. These tolls are seen as forms of extortion, and people submit to police demands only because they are backed up by the threat of violence. Unlike many other forms of corruption, about which Nigerians are more ambivalent because they perceive positive as well as negative dimensions to particular transactions, checkpoint levies are widely viewed as forms of corruption with no redeeming features – except, of course, by the police who collect the money. The problem, of course, is that a population trained into habits of petty bribery find it difficult to argue for distinctions like these when faced with an official's outstretched hand.

Bribery, Corruption, and Social Morality

The examples of everyday bribery in this chapter suggest some of the complexity of the relationship between inequality, corruption, and social morality that can be lost in polemics about the evils of bribery. Corruption is part of an explanation for the dramatic inequalities that characterize Nigerian society, but it is also a strategy to survive in the face of these inequalities. Although cases of favoritism based on social ties sometimes elicit discussions among Nigerians about conflicts of interest, by and large such instances of corruption are accepted because they build on established ideas about acceptable forms of behavior. Relatives helping their kin and patrons assisting their clients are long-standing strategies for navigating social life. Even forms of corruption such as the unwarranted payment for a public service, like my obtaining a driver's license, are widely tolerated because they offer people a means to achieve their objectives in the face of an impersonal, unsympathetic, and often inefficient bureaucracy. A typical strategy in dealing with the state is to try to turn an anonymous encounter into a more personal relationship, so that the official with whom one is dealing is transformed into a provider of favors, and bribes are reconfigured as dashes. Actors on both sides of the exchange are frequently more comfortable operating in a manner that humanizes the transaction between citizen and state.

But it is also true that bureaucratic rules provide opportunities for officials to exploit their positions. Instances of corruption where ordinary citizens are unable to transform their relationships into a more personal idiom provoke anger that is more intense than when favors are personalized. Cases of outright extortion, such as at police checkpoints, are seen as having no redeeming features whatsoever. With the growth in the size and scope of the Nigerian state and the increase in the number of interactions that ordinary people must have with the state in order to achieve their everyday aspirations (for education, health care, jobs, business opportunities, etc.), the chance that encounters with the state will be more impersonal is escalating. Further, the squeeze placed on civil servants by insufficient and delayed salaries, rapid inflation, and the costs associated with achieving their own families' aspirations – all exacerbated by the continuing expectations to help kin, friends, and associates – create immense pressures to be corrupt.

Debates about the boundaries of acceptable corruption are common in popular discourse in Nigeria. In conversations that occur in marketplaces, at bus stops and bars, and in village community halls, national, regional and local politicians are frequently judged by whether they are sharing the benefits of their offices with their people or "eating alone." Ordinary citizens see their leaders as having forsaken the obligations of sharing in favor of personal enrichment and unabashed venality, a fact made more infuriating by the disparity between rich and poor in a country with vast oil wealth.

While Nigeria's mostly poor population has little opportunity to benefit substantially from corruption – indeed it is important to remember that they are its principal victims – it would be a mistake to assume that ordinary citizens have little experience with corruption. As suggested above, the vast majority of Nigerians must interact in one way or another with the state, whether it is to put their children in school, seek health care, pass a police checkpoint on a public highway, vote in an election, or navigate some sort of bureaucratic office for a document necessary for civil or commercial life. As such, most Nigerians have firsthand experience with corruption, and all of the people I know, regardless of their social class, are aware that it is a prominent feature of national life. Because many poor people depend upon the principle of reciprocity between elites and their clients to get access to basic resources, people of all social strata have a vested interest in certain forms of corruption. Ending large-scale corruption, as inimical as it is to ordinary Nigerians' well being, is more difficult because more ordinary forms of corruption are so embedded in everyday life and real progress won't be possible until there are broad and systemic solutions.

Daniel Jordan Smith joined the Department of Anthropology at Brown University in July 2001. He received an AB in Sociology from Harvard University in 1983, an MPH from Johns Hopkins University in 1989, and a PhD in Anthropology from Emory University in 1999. Smith conducts research in Nigeria focusing on a range of issues, including social change, political culture, kinship, and health. He won the 2008 Margaret Mead Award for his book, *A Culture of Corruption: Everyday Deception and Popular Discontent in Nigeria* (Princeton University Press, 2007). His newest book, *AIDS Doesn't Show Its Face: Inequality, Morality, and Social Change in Nigeria* (University of Chicago Press, 2014) examines the social effects of Nigeria's HIV epidemic.

Chapter Ten

What Companies Can't Do About Corruption

Alexandra Wrage

Much of this book has focused on the supply side of corruption, that is, the giver of the bribe. But because bribery is inherently a two-way street, enforcement efforts which tend to punish only the bribe-giver address just part of the problem. This article, which was originally published by Forbes magazine as part of a recurring blog on its website, looks at the demand side of the bribery equation, which is often more pernicious than the supply side. Companies should be aware that for all they can do to curb corruption in their international business transactions on their end, there are some things that simply can't be done about corruption in all respects.

In a coup-prone country in western Africa a few years ago, I heard this story over dinner. A major international development bank had settled on terms for a significant loan to the state for a series of infrastructure projects. The funds arrived and the person telling the story accompanied the Minister of Finance to the main bank. The Minister instructed the teller that there was to be a new and more favorable currency exchange rate for the day and the financial instrument was to be converted at this new rate. Approximately 90% of the total was to be deposited in the State's account and the balance, generated by the more favorable rate, was to be deposited in a second account, for which he slid across the account number. The original exchange rate was then restored.

I don't know if this story is true, but the person with whom I was dining was in a position to know and had little reason to make it up. It didn't reflect well on his organization and so was, as they say, a statement against interest. It probably doesn't matter if it is true; it's still a fine example of how corruption at a certain level is beyond the reach of enforcement agencies and international organizations tasked with increasing international transparency and prosecuting corruption. The right amount of development funds ended up in the right account. The senior official made off with a significant cut, probably after tipping the teller as one might a blackjack dealer. The exchange rate was restored and the lender, if they ever checked, would have found nothing amiss.

The last decade has seen a consistent trend toward greater enforcement of anti-bribery laws against companies and individuals, both by the United States and, with a less steep trajectory, other countries. Whether they're stating it expressly or acting on it quietly, governments are using corporations as their primary tool to reduce international bribery. They alarm companies with vast fines and terrify individuals with substantial prison sentences with the hope of ending the payment of bribes because they cannot, in most cases, do much of anything about those demanding them. This is not inappropriate. Companies are regulated, subject to laws and answerable to shareholders. The worst offenders demanding bribes, on the other hand, do so with impunity, hiding behind sovereign immunity and, often, their own, complicit local law enforcement. Abacha. Suharto. Marcos. Duvalier. It's a longstanding tradition, still thriving in many countries today.

US and some European law enforcement agencies have been extraordinarily successful, with fines in the United States now counted in the billions of dollars and other jurisdictions promising to catch up soon. While these efforts have done more than anything else to reduce bribery, they have yet to convince us that companies are both the sole source and solution of all international corruption — and that's insupportable. There are situations, as in the story above, where the government official isn't just above the rules, he's designing the rules to suit himself. A more typical situation looks like this: a US company is keen to enter into a joint venture with a national oil company to drill for oil in a particularly challenging market. Concerned about the US Foreign Corrupt Practices Act (FCPA), the far-reaching law that criminalizes improper payments to foreign officials, the company hires lawyers and accountants with great expertise in the region. All transactions are scrutinized. All contractors and third parties are vetted. Everyone standing near the transaction is thoroughly and repeatedly trained. The US company, in accordance with the terms in its contract, makes quarterly payments to the national oil company, accounting for everything accurately in its books. At intervals thereafter, the kleptocratic Minister of Petroleum reaches his sticky arm into the state's till and pulls out whatever he needs. Is the US company responsible for this corruption? What about the bank into which the funds were deposited? Or the governments that prop up the grasping leadership? Or the consumers who eventually buy the products far downstream?

Unfortunately, some companies are actively and knowingly participating in bribery because they're impatient for higher sales, they have a shoddy product or they believe it's the only way to do business in some countries. Far more are working to get this issue right: they're broadcasting the right message, implementing appropriate controls and safeguarding their reputation. I will talk about both communities in this new blog, but let's start by agreeing that there is intractable corruption at the highest levels in some states, including a few OECD states, that we can't reach with more prosecutions of multinational companies. The simple reality is that there are just some things that companies can't do about corruption.

Alexandra Wrage is the president of TRACE International. She has written three compliance guidebooks and is the author of *Bribery and Extortion: Undermining Business, Governments and Security,* and the host of the training DVD *Toxic Transactions: Bribery, Extortion and the High Price of Bad Business* produced by NBC. Ms. Wrage has previously served on the Independent Governance Committee (IGC) of the Fédération Internationale de Football Association (FIFA), and as Chair of the Anti-Corruption Committee of the ABA's International Section, and Chair of the International Legal Affairs Committee of the Association of Corporate Counsel. She has also participated in anti-bribery working groups with the OECD and the UN Global Compact. Ms. Wrage was named one of the "Canadians Changing the World" by the *Toronto Globe and Mail* in 2011, and one of Maryland's Top 100 Women for 2012.

Conclusion

A lmost all of the bribery schemes described in this book – real and hypothetical – could have been prevented or at least discovered, had adequate controls been established. But in order to develop adequate controls, companies must first know what to look for. That task can be especially difficult with respect to bribery.

One lesson from the stories collected here is that employees often engage in unethical acts with good intentions. They bend the rules not because they particularly want to, but because they think they need to. Think of Asef Choudhry, the business development manager we met in Chapter Two, who so desperately believed that a deal with Filipino agent Omicrom was his company's only chance to make headway in the Asia-Pacific region. The pressure to win business and save his company caused him to ignore all the obvious red flags and eventually led to his company being investigated by US government authorities.

The misconduct described in this book also arises in part because of poor leadership. We are left to wonder at the end of Chapter One, for example, if Glencore's recent public offering has truly signalled a change in its tone from the top, or whether it's all just window dressing. Tone at the top must be expressed with clarity, and all employees must be made to understand that from the highest to the lowest levels of the company hierarchy, they are expected to act in compliance with ethical and legal standards. "Tone at the top" is the visible willingness by senior management to put ethics at the same level of importance as sales and revenue.

Legal and compliance departments obviously also play a big part. But good compliance programs are effective not because they necessarily fulfill every single item on some magical checklist, but because they are responsive to actual human motivations and business systems. Whistleblower hotlines, internal audit regimes, live trainings, due diligence questionnaires, gifts and hospitality forms — these are simply the tools we use in the compliance field to help steer human actions. But they are rendered useless unless they mirror and account for the ways in which employees already behave.

The compliance officer must therefore be comfortable wearing many different hats, including behavioural psychologist, social anthropologist, systems coordinator, and legal expert. If, for example, your code of conduct and anti-bribery policies are not applicable to day-to-day routine activities, then they will languish. And if eighty percent of your work force speaks only Spanish, then those same policies and procedures should be available in Spanish too. As we saw in Chapter Six, multinational companies must be sensitive to regional risks. Any compliance team operating in China should be aware of the various ways in which travel agencies, prepaid gift cards, and underground banks are used to discreetly pay bribes to government officials.

Good compliance also means listening to your employees. As Musikilu Mojeed remarks in Chapter Seven, a company's on-the-ground staff are often its best form of protection. By engaging local Nigerian employees to conduct an internal investigation of their use of a local agent known for unethical behavior, Panalpina's executives in Houston were able to put a policy in place allowing for only limited use of the third party.

When you create a compliance culture that is in harmony with your business practices, you will see the difference it makes. You will see employees who are engaged in what they're doing and not cynical, who are proud of their company's ethical commitment and who consistently make the right decisions in difficult situations. Compliance can actually become a catalyst for business growth.

Of course, there is always plenty of work to be done in the compliance arena. The business world will never be entirely free of commercial corruption, just as it won't be free of fraud, embezzlement or tax evasion. Markets are global, cultures and economies are diverse, and we face the ongoing challenge of accommodating this diversity in well focused and robust compliance programs. And as we saw in Chapter Ten, there will always be corrupt politicians out there for which nothing can be done.

But compliance teams can put themselves at a competitive advantage just by learning to think like a criminal. There are numerous creative permutations of malfeasance that can exist at a company. But if we can pause to ask ourselves how we would go about paying a bribe within our own organizations, we can more easily spot and fix the weaknesses within our own compliance programs.

Made in the USA
Charleston, SC
16 March 2014